Her Name Is *MERCY*

Her Name Is
MERCY

BY

SISTER MARIA DEL REY
of Maryknoll

CHARLES SCRIBNER'S SONS NEW YORK

To Mother Mary Joseph,

MOLDER OF MISSIONERS
AND A GREAT WOMAN

Contents

The Three-Quarter-Length Coat

Shivering refugees, squatting shoulder to shoulder, packed the narrow alleys like a carpet. They all faced in the same direction —the one point toward which these narrow alleys converged, the point of relief from pain. The Maryknoll Sisters' Clinic in Pusan, Korea, tended the longest charity line in the world, many newsmen had told me.

I stepped along as briskly as I could, lifting my feet often over a sick child lying on the ground as its mother carefully guarded her place in line. Then I mounted a stairway to a garden crisscrossed with narrow paths leading to various low buildings.

The crowd was here, too, the usual restless mass of Asian people pushing and shoving to get what they need so desperately. It was late afternoon; they had waited all day in line. In fifteen years as travelling journalist throughout Asia, I have seen many such crowds. During my work with the Hong Kong *Sunday Examiner*, I all but lived in refugee centers, relief stations, and at that odd little railroad-trestle in Kowloon where hundreds of thousands of exiles from China have crossed over to the Free World.

This crowd, I sensed, was anxious. The lines were not moving. Intense and insistent, they wanted to know, "Why not?"

Then I saw her in the middle of the crowd, a slim tall woman in white, her Maryknoll habit partly covered by a three-quarter-length coat, her hands toying with the stethoscope around her neck. Dust had settled in the tired lines of her face and caked grimly under her sad eyes—the fine Korean dust which blows over Pusan in hot summer and cold winter.

She turned and spoke to a Korean doctor beside her. He cupped his hands shouting to the restless masses. He said in Korean:

"We have no more medicines to give you. We cannot take care of any more today. But the Practicing Virtue Lady (*Su Nyo*, the Korean term for Sister) asks me to tell you that if you will disperse quietly, she will get milk powder to give you for your children."

I marvelled at the effect. I had said to myself, "Elizabeth Reid, you are going to see a first-class riot. These people are going to be mad, really mad. They have waited hours in line; to frustrate them now is dangerous business."

But not so. These people knew the *Su Nyo*. If she said she had no medicines—well, that meant she had given everything she had. There was no suspicion she might be holding back some. No thought of the Black Market where so many relief goods turned up.

That's my point. These thousands of refugees knew her and trusted her implicitly.

I approached the Maryknoll Sister in the three-quarter-length coat. An Army coat, incidentally, dyed black.

"How many patients do you have here, Sister?" I asked.

Sister watched the crowds as they drifted off the compound.

"An average of two thousand people pass through our hands each day. Sometimes we reach twenty-five hundred; sometimes is is below two thousand but the average keeps around that figure."

"How long have you had that stupendous average?"

"One year? Two years? Somewhere between that. Refugees are still pouring into Pusan. Estimates place the population at 1,500,000 now. It was 250,000 before the war, you know."

2

We were walking toward the edge of the compound, now. As she talked, Sister buttoned the coat around her. Night was settling and November, 1953, was cold in Korea.

"What diseases do you find most prevalent?"

"So many! And such serious diseases! Heading the list, maybe, is tuberculosis. Tuberculous bones cripple thousands of children here. We have 350 kiddies in casts alone—350 small children who must be carried here several times a week by their mothers. Poor women! Smallpox is virulent in many of the refugee camps. Whooping cough, too, which is much more serious here than in the States. Malnourished children develop complications of pneumonia with it."

We were at the compound gate now, talking as dusk settled over the once-beautiful garden. A thin wail came from the other side of the metal gate. Without interrupting her discussion of diseases, the Sister pushed open the gate with her foot and stooped over a bundle of newspapers on the road outside. As she picked it up, the newspapers fell away. I saw she had a baby in her hands, a bit of starving humanity, stark naked. Two weeks old? Three weeks? Certainly not more.

"Typhus is another disease we meet very often. But malnutrition in all its forms is the basic trouble with most of our patients."

Still talking, she ran a practiced hand over the baby's withered arms and legs, lifted the head and peered down the open throat. Then she opened her coat and thrust the tiny thing up against her body so that her own warmth might penetrate the wretched little carcass.

"This is something she has done hundreds, yes, thousands of times," I thought. "She does it without even interrupting her train of thought. This is reflex action with her."

We moved away from the gate toward the lights of a small building.

"How do you ever get supplies for so many, Sister?" I said

3

aloud. "Surely, there must often be days like today when you have to tell the people you have no more medicines."

"Not so often, thank God," she said evenly. "We get medicines from the National Catholic Welfare Council, from the Motherhouse at Maryknoll, from generous friends both in the States and here in Korea. Most of the time we have what we need. Indeed, I think God watches our cupboard quite closely. Only now and then, does He let it be bare for just a little while."

We were at the small house now—a crèche for abandoned babies. They were held here just long enough to heal any diseases and get them in condition to be admitted to an orphanage. We stepped inside. Sister took the wee scrap of humanity from the inside of her coat. Once more her doctor's hands felt the arms and legs, gently pulled open the eyes, checked the ears and mouth. Then she went over to a small sink. She turned on the water. Cupping her hands to catch the flow, she poured the water over the infant's head. "I baptize thee in the name of the Father, and of the Son and of the Holy Ghost." There! It was done. This Baby-Unwanted was a Son of God.

For a brief second, the tall slender woman with the tired eyes and dust-grimed face, held the small baby up against her cheek, in silent adoration of the Godhead dwelling now in this starveling. Then she turned him over to the Korean woman who cared for this crèche of abandoned babies. We went outside. Neither of us had said a word about that baby.

"Thanks, Sister," I said. "I think I have enough information now for a story in our Hong Kong *Examiner*. Just one thing. I would like to mention your name."

"My name?" she queried. "Do you think it necessary? Very well. My name is Sister Mercy."

An apartment on Riverside Drive in New York is a long cry from Pusan, Korea, in more ways than one. Elizabeth Reid sat on a footstool facing me, her long Australian arms locked around

4

her knees, her dark eyes glowing as they saw once more that woman in the three-quarter-length coat.

Thirty-ish or maybe on the sunny side of forty, hers is a ravenous mind. She must drink in all experiences, suffer all pain, fill herself with all joy. That is the journalist in her. She is a leader in The Grail, an international platoon of lay women geared for total service to the Church.

"I saw in her," she said slowly, rocking back and forth a little with her eyes half closed,—"I saw in her something like the complete woman, the global mother. Life flowed out from her in blessings. It was the reason for her being. Life flowed out with no sentimentality, no grandiose gestures. To us all—soldiers, generals, journalists, relief workers, Koreans—she gave as simply as a mother dishing out the family mush. What did we ask for? Her time, her medical skill, her strength, her medicines, food and clothing. Because he needed it, she gave to that baby her body's warmth. To us, who needed more, she gave the warmth of her soul.

"Sister Mercy *is* her name."

1

A Bump to Begin

"Beginning again!" Sister Mercy said, speaking half aloud to the darkening clouds outside the plane window as the Northwest Airlines plane neared Korea.

Maybe ending it all, who could tell? Flying into Korea was touchy business in March, 1951. Before leaving Tokyo at eight that morning, the passengers had been told how to bail out of a plane, and had been initiated into using a Mae West jacket, just in case. . . .

Then, almost at Korea in the late morning, the plane had been ordered back to safety in Japan. Enemy aircraft aloft, orders said.

The pilot did not return all the way to Tokyo. Landing on a Japanese airfield, the few passengers—five men and three Maryknoll Sisters—waited five hours for further instructions.

The men were curious about the Sisters, naturally. How come? Was SCAP (Supreme Command of the Allied Powers) allowing civilians to return to Korea? Nine months before, in June, 1950, when the cold war began shooting, all civilians had been evacuated.

A news cameraman paced back and forth in front of the Sisters working up courage to ask. A man from the State Department stopped him. Together they approached the bench at the edge of the runway.

"Patience won out," the Sisters said. Like others, they had made the endless rounds of offices—Government people, Army officers, Ambassador's staff. "Why don't you write to MacArthur himself?" someone had suggested, half laughing. Well, they did. And shortly after, came SCAP's august permission to return to Korea for the purpose of opening a dispensary to care for refugees. And here they were, the first women civilians permitted to set foot in Korea since the war broke out nine months before.

The talk drifted into silence. No one had much interest in anything except getting on with the journey. The men smoked one cigarette after another, hoping at every puff to get the word which would make each gladly throw his cigarette on the concrete, stamp it out and start toward the plane. The Sisters once again buried their noses in prayer books, looking up at the end of each psalm for signs of a hurried order to leave.

At last it came. "Proceed on to Pusan. You have a good chance to make a run for it now." Five men and three Sisters filed again into the stuffy plane cabin, and the doors banged shut. With the whirr of the propellers, the last inclination to talk died down. Sister Mercy lapsed into the state of mind of most Sisters when alone, midway between thinking and praying with perhaps a tiny edge on the thinking.

People are usually at a loss to describe Sister Mercy. Not tall and slender; not short and fat. Not beautiful; not bad looking. Not fair nor yet dark. I usually end up saying, "Well, God has been awfully generous to her; big eyes, big nose, big mouth, big frame, big heart. Nothing niggardly about her. Nothing tight and hard. And yet nothing loose. Everything is big but her voice, which is surprisingly soft and low. She seems expandible, somehow. She swells out to take in everybody, talking easily to a cardinal, a general, a visiting Lady Somebody-or-Other; matching knowledge to knowledge with a medical commission; and turning very simply to a broken-down old man who wants twenty-

7

five cents and knows where to get it. She sees in everybody exactly the same thing—a body made by God and a soul redeemed by Him."

The usual four-hour flight from Tokyo to Pusan on the southern tip of Korea was lengthening out to an all-day grind. But please God, six o'clock should see them landing in beloved Korea. Korea again! Beloved, beloved Korea!

Why should she be so exultant at this return to Korea? Hadn't she told them all in the Beni (and meant it, too) that she was leaving her heart in Boliva's jungle lands?

Seven years there in Boliva! The hard work of setting up a hospital in the rubber and brazil-nut country was just past. They were good years as a doctor would reckon them, each day filled with large black eyes pleading for relief from suffering. Women with tangled hair and betel-blackened teeth, eager and yet afraid to hear what Madre-Doctora had to say about Pedrito's chance for life. Men with dull eyes and hollow cheeks. Their blood counts made the lab technician check and check again to see if she hadn't made a mistake. Haemoglobin: 20%, 15%, 10 and even 5%.

"But Sister!" a new Sister-nurse had protested. "I'm sure there's something wrong with this report. 15% haemoglobin? Why in nursing school the text books said 50% is very, very low."

"These are ignorant, suffering people, Sister dear," Sister Mercy had soothed her. "They don't know what your textbook says. They just keep right on living and sometimes, with God's help, we are able to bring them back to 25 or 30%, which is fairly usual here."

"And in the States we get excited when it hits 60%!" The tyro was chagrined.

Yes, in Bolivia's jungle land men and women do a hard day's work at 30%. If big blustery Americans knew that, how many of them would talk of "laziness" and "manana land"? Malaria and hookworms accounted for those white tongues, lack-luster eyes and low haemoglobin percentages. "All my life I've been

8

fighting such measly things—mosquitoes and worms! Ah well, who am I to match my strength with something big?"

But there had been big things to fight too—things to challenge any doctor or surgeon. Cases were brought to the little hospital after days of jogging through the jungle carried on a hammock slung from a shoulder pole—jaguar clawings, ugly wounds from "tigre" traps, a man whose leg had been crunched off by an alligator, another poor fellow half-squeezed to death by a boa constrictor. That was where the hard work was—he was only half-squeezed.

Yes, the seven years in Bolivia had been full. Plenty of work for her *materia medica*, her surgeon's knife, her cool hands and warm smile. Full, vigorous, mission years, but Sister Mercy's first love was Korea.

She roused herself to look about the plane. Each of the men had taken a seat to himself. Four of them slept; only one industriously ruffled his papers. The other two Sisters sat in front of her, their black-veiled heads turned to each other in animated conversation.

Most of the seats up front had been removed and the space was piled high with cargo shrouded in canvas. "Army supplies urgently needed, I suppose. Can't wait for regular Army service. We will have to be getting rush supplies on this plane, too, in the future. I'd better check at the airport and find out what their schedule is. And when I get it I'll have to translate it into Korean for the benefit of our helpers at the dispensary. That's something new; in the old days, plane schedules were unknown to Korea—at least in our missions up north."

How much of the language was left to her? Looking out on the late March afternoon sky, the silvery whirr of the propeller blades no longer glistening in the sun, she smiled to think of those dogged hours of study twenty years before. So much hard work, just to be able to say,

"Where does it pain you?"

"How old is the baby?"

9

"Take three of these every day with a glass of water." Only they didn't have glasses.

First, she had studied to pass the Japanese Medical Board tests to qualify as a physician in Korea. Japan was Lord of Korea in the 1930's and insisted on the right papers.

Internship? St. Francis Hospital, La Crosse, Wis., U.S.A. Right!

Medical School? Marquette University, Milwaukee, U.S.A. Right!

High School? Cathedral High School, Milwaukee, U.S.A. Right!

Grammar School? Saints Peter and Paul, Milwaukee, U.S.A. Right!

Kindergarten? None.

A potent silence followed this. Sucking in his breath the official had released it slowly, in a long-drawn Sa-a-a-a-ah! An unfilled blank might be serious for him when checked by higher-ups. Pen poised, he looked up.

"No kindergarten?"

Sister Mercy felt her heart sink. "No," she said. And thought, "Will I have to make up my kindergarten credits before they let me practice medicine in Korea?"

But the papers went through. She was summoned to Japan, took the Medical Board examinations in Tokyo and, in due time, received a license to practice medicine in Japan and its possessions.

After that hurdle, there was a bigger one—the language. It took hard plugging. Four and five hours a day putting tongue and throat muscles through their paces. By night she felt that her whole personality had taken a beating.

Then came the big assignment—a dispensary to open in Sinweiju, called in Japanese "Shingishu," or "New Gishu." Old Gishu was some twelve miles away, not directly on the railroad which Japan had built as a backbone running down the peninsula. Shingishu was a spanking new town, right on the railroad where it crossed the Yalu River over into Antung in Manchuria. The railroad was Japan's modern touch but it was much nicer in wintertime, when one could cross the Yalu by sleigh. From November until March the river was the smoothest highway in Korea or Manchuria.

But for all its newness, perhaps because of it, Shingishu had few conveniences to offer. Sister Mercy found herself installed in a tiny dispensary tucked under the church steps. Equipment? One chair, one table, a few shelves and four kinds of medicines. Not even a waiting room! The crowds jostled each other outside in summer and crowded into the treatment room itself in winter. Nevertheless, some 1,500 patients per month passed under her hands. She spent two years under the church steps before the new dispensary was built attached to the convent. Oceans of room, it seemed to her, with waiting room, treatment room, small pharmacy and even an office of sorts. And all brave with white paint.

Those days in northern Korea she was out more than she was in, it seemed. House calls brought her to nearly every section of town. Luckily the convent was at the hub where the Chinese, Korean and Japanese sections came to a common point. Then there were weekly visits to Hiken with the hundred-or-so patients who were there waiting for treatment each week.

She had the First Communion class, too. It was a real test to teach these little children; about twenty of them were in the class. Their bright striped sleeves were no brighter than the shoe-button eyes and the quick smiles.

The diseases were pretty uniform. Impetigo, malaria, dysentery, and—always—worms. Children with flies in their ears; children with tuberculous bones; children with swollen tummies and gaunt cheeks. But always with that gentle dignity in suffering she came to recognize as innately Korean.

The diseases were constant. The floods and fires were added suffering. The big flood of '35 for instance! She had been in Manchuria, across the river, when the dikes around the city were threatened. City-folk who could afford to pay the rents inside the city were saved, but the thousands who clustered just outside the city limits were swept away. Sister Mercy came back a day or so later, wading up to her knees in mud through the streets.

Eighty women and children were sheltered in the church basement. The yard was full of wood, fires and cooking pots, and hectic women. Sister Luke and Sister Agnita ran the sewing machine day and night, sewing up clothes from sample materials sent from the States. Outside, another Sister had quite an operation going at the water hydrant. A line-up of children took turns splashing around and soaping themselves. After the bath, she gave each a set of clean clothes and some food.

The Sodality women and girls were all over the place, cooking food, settling arguments among the refugees, and straightening out whose children did what to whom. It was at ten that night that the doorbell rang and Agatha (good, dependable, truly Christ-like Agatha!) stood in the doorway with two children.

"Their mother died this afternoon," Agatha said. "I found them crying over the dead body in one of the matsheds down by the dike. The father left six months ago to look for work, and the poor mother had been trying to make a living for them all by selling pancakes along the road."

The two girls, nine and seven years old, were bathed and fed and clothed, and went to join the other children asleep out on the front porch.

So many many cases! They crowded into her mind. The family she had visited—parents, two children and grandmother. She took care of the sick mother and was just about to go when something desperate in the father's eye prompted her to ask, "When did you eat last?" The story came out; nobody in that house had eaten for three days. No fuel in the house, either, and that was December 18th.

Old Ngu Kim complained of "awful noises in my head." He would not be satisfied until Sister Mercy had run the stethoscope from ear to ear and back to front over his scalp. "Ah, much better now," he had murmured. "I knew that was what I needed."

Ignorance, which took more harmful forms than that of old Ngu Kim, was perhaps the biggest obstacle. Baths were taboo; vegetables and good eating habits were scorned. Sometimes, as she went out the front door, the devil doctor came in the rear door. It all took quiet perseverance, patience, genuine love for the poor and (which always came with that love) understanding of why they acted as they did.

Gradually the prejudice broke down. In 1933, children had run after the Sisters in the streets, calling, "Western big nose!" "Foreigners!" Two years later, they came smiling, "*Su Nyo*, I need medicine for my mother."

Even in normal times (if the Japanese occupation could be considered "normal"), the Koreans seemed always to be climbing out of one disaster when they were hit by another. In 1939, it was the rice crop's failure. Those were the days when Sister Mercy's asthma was so bad that she was told to return to the States the next year. She returned—and was caught in the aftermath of Pearl Harbor, unable to get back to Korea. The years in Bolivia had followed then.

Sister Mercy shook herself. No more dreaming of the past. Let's look to the future. After eleven years she was returning to Korea, but how differently! In 1940, she had taken a slow boat to Japan and sailed from there to the States on a Pacific liner. Now in 1951, she was flying back in an American plane. In 1940, she had left the North; it was now entirely under Russia. She was returning to the South which she had never seen. In 1940, she had left an oppressed country; in 1951, she returned to a nation split asunder for six years. Worse still, it was now mangled in the teeth of Russia, snapping to grab a bigger bite, while the United Nations clung like a bull-dog to the South. Korea's blood ran red from the jaws of both of them. Her job, by permission of SCAP, was to staunch that blood.

13

Thanks be to God, she would have a fine team to work with. Affectionately, she viewed the two black veils showing above the double seat ahead of her. Viewed from the rear, there is nothing so impersonal as a head draped in nun's black veiling. There's no character to it; just a black roundness.

The back of most women's heads tell you something about the person. A tilt of the hat, a mass of blond hair, a precise haircut at the neckline—one can guess the personality. But the back of a nun's head? It's a complete blank.

Who could guess that those two black round things peeping over the back of the seats ahead, were the outer casings of two very spry brains? And, just by looking at them, who would know that those brains were at the command of two stout hearts eager to face any trials to help the suffering poor? Already they had faced plenty.

The black round thing on the right was the head of Sister Rose of Lima, nurse and pharmacist from Jersey City, New Jersey, veteran and dear companion of those Shingishu days. She spoke Korean, of course; indeed, she'd been evacuated from Pusan just nine months before, when war broke out in June, 1950.

The round black thing on the left was the head of Sister Augusta, a nurse from Meadville, Pennsylvania. Tried and true, too. Fifteen years in China had confirmed her as a missioner. She, too, had been evacuated to Japan the previous June, after only a few months in Pusan. The language would be difficult for her, of course. But already she had a fair hold on it. The months of waiting in Japan had not been idle. One could count on Sister Augusta, with her quick wit and ready smile, to be a strong staff for this pioneering venture—no doubt about it.

The others would follow within a week, travelling by boat with the heavy baggage, the medicines, the instruments, the big things one would need for a clinic. One would be Sister André, another old-timer in Korea. She, too, had been in Shingishu in the early days—there and in other Korean missions. Later she had gone to Manchuria to work among the Koreans. Through

14

it all she had never lost her old Kentucky drawl. A business woman to her finger tips! She could be counted upon to see the baggage through customs without losing a single nail from any crate.

The other would be Sister Agnus Therese, a young doctor fresh from Maryknoll, a real tyro on the missions. She ought to be a big help to Sister Mercy. "I'm getting along; I'm all of forty-eight," she murmured to herself. "I'm the Grandmother-doctor of Maryknoll, the first of our Sisters to practice medicine."

These five on the medical team would be together in Korea. In Japan was another young Sister, Sister Alberta Marie from Detroit, Michigan, a teacher, straining at the leash to come. She would wait for the seventh team-mate to join her from the Philippines. This last was Sister Herman Joseph a laboratory technician from Salem, Oregon, one of the corps of pre-war Korean missioners who had been scattered by the war. She had spent the last five years at a hospital set in the sugar-cane fields of Occidental Negros. She was to go to Japan and then the last two members of the team would come to Pusan together, within a few months. A real gathering of the clan from the ends of the earth.

All good men and true, the team leader said to herself. The words of a letter she had written to Maryknoll just the night before—had they really been in Japan just last night?—came to mind. "I feel we are launching out into the great unknown. It is not going to be easy. I hope only that God's Will be accomplished in us."

Lights streamed past the window. The other passengers were leaning over to collect odd bits of baggage here and there. With a soft bounce, the plane hit the ground and rolled awkwardly along the runway.

Sister Mercy unbuckled her seat belt and began assembling her belongings—the microscope case at her feet, umbrella overhead, the purse beside her. She stood up and stretched. Korea at last! It was the longest period of sitting she was to have for the next five years.

2

Carpet of Pain

Sister Rose of Lima clung to the windowsill in the bus and gasped. It was a rickety old bus, too ancient to have been commandeered by the Army. Sister Rose of Lima rubbed the murk off the window and stared at what was once familiar territory, and was now so changed.

The bus was whizzing along the fifty-minute road from the airfield to the Northwest Airlines office in the city of Pusan. That was normal enough, since the commercial airline had discontinued service into Seoul and was using Pusan as its Korean terminal in 1951. But as she remembered Pusan nine months before, there was no smooth road out of the city; there was no airport for it to go to—just a temporary runway; most of all, there were no hundreds and thousands of jeeps, weapon carriers, and trucks pushing past with glaring headlights.

Nine months ago when Sister Augusta, Sister André and she had been evacuated to Japan, this had been a quiet agricultural section. Small homes, rice paddies, an occasional ox, a green mountain or two—that sort of thing. But now they passed acres of army supplies: fields piled high with truck tires; cartons of food stacked up like the Tower of Babel; motor pools filled with jeeps, jeeps and more jeeps; ammunition dumps surrounded by high barbed wires and WARNING! signs in all languages; Army tents and Navy quonsets, derricks and cranes, bulldozers, tanks,

16

mobile guns and radar sets; shoe laces, chewing gum, typewriter ribbons, crackers, cheese snacks—

"I see the G.I. has arrived in force," she said turning from the window.

"It's nothing like the Pusan we left last June, that's certain," Sister Augusta concurred.

Now and then the headlights picked up groups of people standing by the roadside waiting for the bus to pass. They seemed to be family groups all laden with buckets, bundles, baskets. Weary people and ragged, but firm in the stoicism of those who have set their faces toward a destination and will not be turned aside.

The bus was entering the city now, heading for the Airlines office. The old narrow streets could not be changed overnight just because another war had broken out. The bus slowed as it moved carefully along the dark streets. At first they seemed deserted, but as speed reduced to a mere crawl, Sister Rose of Lima took note of them.

A dark huddle in the doorway! Why, that was a woman sleeping. A heap of old clothes right on the pavement twitching in several places at once was several children (four? five?) bedded down there under an overcoat and sweaters, keeping one another warm. A cardboard carton in a slit between buildings! There was a man's head protruding out one side and his legs came out the other. Was this all the house he had? A baby wailed sharply behind a piece of tattered canvas tacked up on a crazy framework. A woman rocked it and put it to her dry breast. But a baby will scream when it is hungry.

Further in the downtown section the sidewalk sleepers were closer together. They overflowed the street and ran over the curb. Finally they left just enough room for the bus to pass. It was true. The city was carpeted with human misery Sister Rose of Lima turned from the window. Her eyes met Sister Augusta's.

"How many of them are there, do you think?"

"Thousands and thousands! The poor people!" Sister Augusta's voice was awed.

"Hundreds of thousands is nearer the truth," remarked Father Craig. A Maryknoll priest twenty-five years in Korea, he had met the Sisters at the airport.

"Really, Father? As many as that?" Sister Mercy queried.

"No one can estimate it exactly, of course," Father Craig said. "But the city has at least doubled in its Korean population alone. That doesn't count the thousands and thousands of United Nations troops pouring in. Let's see what that means in terms of American cities. Pusan had 250,000 people before this 'incident.' That is just about equal to the population of Dayton; Omaha; Long Beach, California; Oklahoma City; or Providence. It's a bit bigger than Syracuse, New York."

"And a bit smaller than my home town of Jersey City," put in Sister Rose of Lima.

"Right! With that population Pusan had its own ratio of very poor people. Remember, Korea was dominated by the Japanese. There were few rich Koreans. Now suppose that in the States, Dayton suddenly found all of Omaha was trekking into it, bringing only the rags on their backs? What would be the condition of Dayton after nine months? How about water, housing, garbage disposal, food, sanitary facilities?

"Suppose Providence went to live with Syracuse and brought nothing with it? Suppose Oklahoma City moved in with Long Beach?

"Then remember that hundreds of thousands of troops have landing here, staying for various lengths of time and moving on to the battlefields. They bring their own food and housing, thanks be to God—indeed, they provide employment, which helps—but they do take up space. Army vehicles, Army hospitals, Army supplies naturally have top priority for available land. Rice paddies, vegetable plots, pasture lands are used up.

"The figure I gave you as the present estimate of refugees here is just that—the estimate as of now. Tomorrow it will be higher

18

by a couple of thousands. Everyday the city is more and more crowded." He was silent for a moment. "And they don't arrive in Cadillacs."

"So I see," Sister Mercy murmured. "Thousands, hundreds of thousands. Each one a suffering body and a bewildered soul. Dear Lord, and we are so few!"

"Don't lose heart now, Sister," Father Craig went on. "The job is only beginning. This city's population will reach a million and a half within a year's time. And five out of every six persons you'll see on the street will be destitute strangers. Imagine such a situation in a city the size of Cleveland, Boston, St. Louis or Baltimore! Besides," he smiled a wry smile, "Pusan had always had its own destitute. Medical care for them was scanty even before this hit them."

"We know," Sister Augusta and Sister Rose of Lima agreed. "We were starting a clinic to help them here when the war broke out and we had to leave."

Sister Mercy was, as always, practical and cheerful. "We're not much help but thank God we're here!"

The bus had jerked to a stop. An excited jabber of Korean broke out from the sidewalk. Three women and a man showed up in front of the Airlines office, jumping up and down, waving their hands at the nuns and priest.

"Agada! And Patrisya! Pellado! Nita, too!"

It was a grand reunion! Eleven years had passed since Agada had last seen Sister Mercy in Shingishu—eleven years of World War II, the Russian occupation of the city and now the Korean war. Agada, the faithful, had cooked for the Sisters in Gishu first, and had come to the Shingishu house in May, 1935. Seven years later she saw them off to an internment camp and later sent back to the States. Three years of war followed. Japan, the master-nation, was losing out, which did not make things easier for the conquered Koreans. Then came Russia in one fast swoop from the north in 1945.

Agada escaped, but it was not easy. In North Korea, the

19

phrase "I think I'll slip over the border tonight" can be classed among Famous Last Words. It is a dangerous pastime in any Communist country. Agada did it, though, and got her niece Patrisya out, too. Together, they went south to Seoul and lived there for some years managing an orphanage. News that Mary-knoll Sisters were to open a dispensary in Pusan filtered up to Agada in Seoul. She packed her bags and came on the run. Hardly had the Sisters landed in December, 1949, when she was knocking at the door, all ready to stay forever, if needed. All three Sisters in Pusan at the time were old Shingishu-ites. Sisters Rose Genevieve, Rose of Lima and André dropped everything and sat down for an evening of catching up on the past seven years' news. Six months later, when the Sisters were evacuated to Japan in June, 1950, Agada and Patrisya, the ever-faithful ones, stayed in the house to protect it.

Nita, a Korean version of Rita, was a nurse. It was she who had helped in the short-lived dispensary operating from April until the evacuation in June. It was she and Patrisya who had brought necessary supplies like food and clothes to Haileah where Americans were detained to await evacuation ships to Japan. It was only two days' waiting at Haileah, but to see their beaming faces at the compound gate had been reassurance that they would return somehow.

And now, on the return to Pusan, the Sisters saw more than three Korean women and one Korean man in the little delegation waving in excitement. It was the first enthusiastic offer of help from the very nation itself. Americans and Koreans would band together to aid these unfortunate hundreds of thousands. A small beginning, but enthusiastic. Maybe only a drop in the bucket, but at least a drop. A drop of the right stuff can be very powerful.

Just then Nita furnished the right drop of the right stuff. "The clinic is still open," she announced. "Every day, Doctor Rhee and I take care of patients, as many as we can. Supplies are very hard to get, especially when one is Korean and nobody official. But now you are here. . . ." Her eyes glowed!

Later over a chicken dinner (something almost unheard of in Pusan those days) priest, Sisters and Koreans discussed the situation and what they hoped to do about it.

The Maryknoll Sisters' property there consists of several acres on a steep hillside. Indeed, the hillside seems to rush down to the street at breakneck speed. The street runs at the base of the hill. In leveling it off, it had been necessary to cut into the hill. Consequently, the property met the street with a steep cliff scaled by some twenty steps or so.

Two houses were on it, built by Nakamura San—a Japanese gentleman more interested in his garden than in living indoors. Close to the street was a house of stone, square, blunt and with a mansard roof. Two rooms upstairs and two downstairs were all that belonged to the "foreign house" proper. But a heterogeneous collection of one-story wings surrounded the lower floor, all built of wood and badly in need of paint. The other house, perched halfway up the property, was an exquisite Japanese house of wood consisting of one large room and two tiny ones, more like alcoves partitioned off with sliding doors. The living quarters were small; Nakamura San had lived in his garden.

The property had been a showplace in Pusan in pre-World War II. Post-war Korea, however, was not a healthy climate for Japanese. The owner had had to return to Japan; his beautiful garden was taken into custody as Alien Property. Five years of neglect and now nine months of war, famine and no-place-to-live, had ruined his work. It was just as well that Nakamura San could not see it.

"Twenty Carmelite Sisters from Seoul are living in the little house up the hill," Father Craig explained. "Another group, the Sisters of Our Lady of Perpetual Help, are in the upper floor of the 'foreign house,' sleeping on the floor at night, using the rooms for dining, recreation and work. Twenty French Fathers have just moved out so that you can have accommodations some

21

place in your own property. Also some fifty or sixty people are living in the various buildings around the place. Oh yes, I forgot the dogs, Teddy and Buster—and a cat."

"Teddy here? He was just a pup when we left," said Sister Augusta.

"Not just *a* pup; he was Sister André's pup," Sister Rose of Lima put in. "When she knows he's here waiting for her, she can sing her *Nunc Dimittis*. Life can hold no further joy for her."

"Teddy has been faithful to her," Father reported. "For months now he's taken a stand outside the convent, like the Faithful Fido of fiction."

"Let's get on with outlining the situation," came from Sister Mercy.

"The garden is used, too," Father continued. "You see, all the schools have been converted into hospitals for wounded soldiers of all nations. Teachers must find some more-or-less quiet spot on a mountainside, or in some side street where they can hold class. Well, there are eight school classes congregating in your garden."

Sister Mercy smiled. "That's fine!" she said, rubbing her hands together. "We'll be one big happy family together. I'm only glad we had the space to give them."

"Now that we've taken care of the past and present," suggested Sister Rose of Lima, "let's get on to the future. When can we start caring for those poor people we saw tonight?"

"Let's see," Sister Mercy pulled a calendar from her pocket. "Today's March 19th, Monday—Monday of Holy Week. We have to check in with the UN officials and the Government people. Then Holy Week services at the end of the week!

"Sister André and Sister Agnus Therese are to sail with the medical supplies soon and it will take about a week for them to get here. They ought to arrive around the 31st. Once the supplies are here it shouldn't take long to set up the clinic, especially if we have everything cleaned and ready for them. Yes, April 2nd,

two weeks from today, should be our opening date for the en-
larged clinic."

And so it was done!

Army nurse Frances Register was just about at the end of her
rope. She had seen much in her four months in Korea.

Besides, she was really sick. The nurses' quarters were cold
and drafty; she had one bad cold after another. The hospitals
were only Korean school buildings, adapted hastily for medical
work. The wounded kept coming in from the north. Sick or well,
the nurses had to stay on their feet.

"Wounded, wounded, wounded!" Frances muttered as the
ambulances drew up to the doors in a seemingly endless stream.
So many young bodies broken, so many minds askew, so many
futures shattered.

It was almost worse when she escaped for a breath of air outside the hospital. The poor people, hungry and cold; the children, grabbing at dirty crusts in the sewer-like gutters. It hurt
her all the more that she saw herself well fed and clad in heavy
woolen clothing and sturdy boots. She wanted to help the
Koreans but just didn't know how to begin.

Then, relations with her fellow nurses began to hit snags. Eight
of them lived in a small room. Tempers flared over trifles, bicker-
ings over drinking, over too much dancing, over this man or
that dress. She was weary of it all.

"Guess I've had a pretty sheltered existence," she told herself.
"I just don't know how to face life—if you call this 'life.'"

Something snapped on Holy Saturday afternoon. "I've got to
get flowers," she insisted to her friend, Captain Ethel Little.
"We should have flowers on the altar for Easter. I've got to
get them."

She knew she must be a little out of her mind. Why be so
insistent about flowers today? She had never been so anxious
to beautify the altar before. But—as she said later—"God and

I were talking together quite often in those days. He knew what was going to happen."

They looked around for a male escort; Army regulations—no nurse was to leave the compound without an armed male escort. Finally, they took off without one.

Miles through the filth and mud of Pusan. No flowers anywhere. They did find a few flower seeds and bought them—foolishly perhaps—as the nearest approach to flowers in all the town. They spoke not a word of Korean.

"Maybe," Frances thought, "maybe if I could talk to somebody who speaks English. . . ."

PUSAN CATHOLIC CHURCH

The sign confronted them across the muddy street. They crossed quickly and entered the dark silent building.

A Korean nun was arranging the altar for Easter services. She stepped down the aisle backwards viewing the effect of the artificial flowers in the sanctuary. The Army nurses touched her on the shoulder.

Without a word, she led them across the court, into a dark building and up steep dark steps. Then a Japanese wall panel opened and there stood a Korean priest. He spoke broken English.

"Reverend Father, we are looking for flowers," Frances stammered.

He bowed as if in apology that he could not oblige her. "Korea is a poor, cold country," he replied. "I am sorry but there are no flowers anywhere at this time of the year."

It was definitely the end of the flower-hunting trail. Frances was silent. Then she looked up quickly.

"Aren't there any American nuns in Korea? It seems to me I heard that Maryknoll Sisters used to be here in Pusan."

"Oh yes," he answered gravely. "Just two days ago, three of them came back."

"Where! Where!" the girls shouted.

24

The priest tried to give directions but they had no idea of street names. "I'll send a boy with you," he decided.

They ran after the young lad. Through alleys, off-limits areas, falling into mud, wading through noisome ditches. Finally their guide whisked up some narrow steps and through a low gate. They followed and found themselves in a run-down Japanese garden. The boy disappeared. Only a Japanese house confronted them.

"The Maryknollers must live here," Ethel said. "Shall we knock?"

They were caked in mud from the waist down. Their shoes were heavy with it. "We can't, we just can't see them like this!" she ended.

"Come on!" Frances urged. "We'll just say that the priest sent us."

She knocked at the door. Sister Rose of Lima answered.

That was all. Frances Register had found a place in Korea where she fitted. From then on, every spare moment was spent helping at the Clinic.

3

Diary of Doings on Mat Shed Hill

MONDAY, APRIL 2. *This morning we unpacked the medicines and equipment which Sister André and Sister Agnus Therese brought with them when they arrived by boat on Saturday. It was strenuous work but we made good headway on it.*

Our good friends, the Korean Sisters of Perpetual Help, now refugees living here, pitched in and helped. The twenty of them cleaned and scrubbed, hauled tables around, set up sterilizers and even built makeshift examining tables and treatment chairs. They are well named; we don't say yet that their help will be perpetual, but we have found it unfailing so far.

Even before we arrived, these Sisters had the house cleaned; the clothes we left behind in the evacuation were washed and ironed. Of course, knowing us from the old days in Pyongyang, they knew how we do things. They are earning a living in various ways. Some work in the Korean military hospitals; some go out to work in the Marine laundry. Others stay here doing embroidery—souvenir towels and hankies for the American boys to send home.

TUESDAY, APRIL 3. *More work on the shipment and getting the place set up to handle medical work.*

In the afternoon, Sister Agnus Therese went up the mountainside to see a young girl sick with pneumonia. She found her in a

26

crazy shelter made of a piece of straw matting supported by tree branches and some cardboard cartons salvaged from the dump heap. Lying on the ground, of course. Nice place for a pneumonia patient in rainy April. Temperature 104 for the past fifteen days; typhoid, pneumonia and asthma complications.

WEDNESDAY, APRIL 4. Raining today, and Sister Mercy went on a sick call up the mountain in back of us. Crowds just naturally accumulate at the sight of a stranger. Sister saw a chance to get to work immediately—not to wait until we have things ready here at home. She took over one of the refugee matsheds, made of straw matting propped up with driftwood. "It was a thrilling clinic," she says. "Nearly everyone needs treatment. Mostly malnutrition and skin diseases." She plans to work here in the dispensary in the morning and go out to her matshed clinic in the afternoons.

Whole families, or usually what are left of them, live in sheds, if they are lucky enough to have one. Others have dug caves in the clay hillsides. Not entire caves really, but shallow depressions which give some protection from wind and rain. Life begins and ends in these holes where sick and well must huddle together. You may think of the Infant Savior born in a cave, or you may think of His first home as a stable-shed. Either way you will gain a clear idea of His poverty at Pusan. The Lord's example has been followed by many small Koreans born here.

Sister Agnus Therese went out to see her patient again. Sister Mercy went with her. When they got back, they regaled us with stories of the slippery wet yellow clay. "It's impossible to keep one's footing on it," Sister Mercy said. "I reached the top only by slipping back two steps for every three I took up."

"It's bad enough for us," Sister Agnus Therese remarked, "but think what it must be for those who live in it, rain or shine. They don't have a dry house to come to at the end of such a jaunt."

Sister Mercy writes home:

April 4, 1951

There will be plenty to do. I can see our work will grow to great proportions. The big problem will be—how to get supplies. I'll cable Father Wycislo of NCWC today. He may have some way to get them to us. As it is, we have to rely on individual men coming on the boats who have offered to bring medicine and things for us.

I have much to tell but I'll wait until I'm more wide awake. As it is, I'm falling asleep over the paper. I know you are praying for us. I can feel it. The needs of the poor people are so very great; I only hope and pray that we may truly become instruments of God's mercy and love.

THURSDAY, APRIL 5. Clinic is open today. The people don't know about us yet so there were only about one hundred. Awfully sick people, though. Dysentery, malaria, pneumonia, but mostly skin diseases and malnutrition. The babies wring one's heart; they are literally starving to death.

If the refugees don't know about us yet, the Army and Navy does! As we go along the crowded streets, American boys come up to ask us who we are and why we came. Several Army nurses, Lt. Frances Register and Captain Little, have been coming every few days helping to paint and scrub. They first saw us on Holy Saturday just four days after we landed. They had come looking for flowers to use in the Army Post chapel on Easter. Were they surprised to see American Sisters! Especially as we are a medical team sent to aid the refugees.

Father Rush, chief of chaplains in this area, has been a friend from the beginning, too. We went to see him on Holy Thursday; on Easter Sunday he spoke of our work at all the Masses in the Post Chapel. Since then, soldiers and sailors, civilian employes, doctors and nurses have been dropping in with offers to help. There's nothing like the Americans for rushing to help the needy!

Chaplain Rosen looked worried as he took a chair in the Chief of Chaplains' office.

"What's the matter?" Father Rush asked. "Haven't you got everything you need for the Passover services?"

"Everything; and then, some!" grunted the rabbi. "Too much. Far too much. The quartermaster must think this whole United Nations army is going to celebrate Passover. They sent cases and cases of matzos."

Just then the Korean houseboy came in dutifully emptying the ashtrays. Chaplain Rosen watched him thoughtfully.

"I only wish the Koreans were Jews," he said. "That boy looks as though he could stand a good meal with matzos."

"Well, why not?" urged the chief. "I know just the place for those extra matzos. They could use the crates and the cardboard cartons, too. You come with me!"

And that was the beginning of the matzos epic at the Mary-knoll Sisters' Clinic in Pusan.

Farmers say that everything of the pig can be used, except the squeal. It was something like that with those famous matzos crates. The nails were carefully pulled out and set aside; the boards were stacked neatly. The crates were made into houses for the help. The cartons, flattened out, went to build many a refugee's matshed; the tarpaper became waterproof roofing; the cardboard boxes went to the pharmacy to hold small medicine bottles, and to the admitting office to stack the file cards in.

The cellophane bags were the last covering. "Very far down to the food!" commented the Korean helpers who felt they had been digging a long time to get to essentials. These were opened, the matzos pressed down, and the vacant space filled with small bags of powdered milk, peanut butter, rice and other staples—whatever was on hand.

And thus it was that thousands of Koreans celebrated Passover with gratitude to Jewish and Catholic chaplains working together!

But the matzos gift spread its wings of mercy far beyond the

Jewish holy days. Boards from the crates were put in as flooring for the whole Clinic. Up to then, the place had been floored with tatami, the Japanese rice-straw matting. Very nice to look at and comfortable underfoot, but not so easy to scrub and disinfect.

Frances Register, on hands and knees, wriggled halfway through the narrow doorway. Then she lay down on her back on the ground. From the waist up, she was in the hot, smelly hut; her legs stretched outside in the warm Spring sunshine.

"Is this how you want me?" she asked Sister Agnus Therese who was cramped beside a sick woman lying someplace there in the semi-darkness. " 'Stasia is out in the yard. There's no room for her here and besides, I think she needs the air."

"Yes," Sister replied. "If you can do it, Frances, will you mix this penicillin? Rather awkward to do when you are lying on your back, but I don't see how else you can fit into this shed."

"With you around, Sister," Frances replied valiantly, "I can do anything! Hand me the cup and things."

It was an odd situation. The doctor on her knees beside the incoherent patient; the nurse on the flat of her back mixing the penicillin. And both of them trying not to mind the flies clustering thick on the woman's sores, the tell-tale traces of rats, the horrible smells.

The treatment was soon over. Leaving the patient a bit more comfortable, Sister and Frances came creeping out of the low doorway in the straw matshed. Twenty or so children stood around.

"Where's 'Stasia?"

"Don't know, Sister. She was right here when I went in. Oh, look at these children!"

More than half of them had full-blown small pox. Flies were crawling over the sores, flitting from one face to another, bringing infection as fast as they could go. Ulcers and running sores,

30

tattered clothes, indescribable thirst. Truly these children were miserable.

"American girl over there," they pointed. "Sick!"

Indeed poor 'Stasia was being sick.

"I can't take it," she explained between retchings. "Too horrible. Too awful. I want so to help, but I can't. That's all, I can't."

Later, safe and clean in the nurses' quarters, 'Stasia looked long at Frances. "Listen," she said, "I'll give money and I'll pray for this work, but I can't bring myself to get into it personally. I have only admiration for those who can. But you ought to take a bit of precaution, too. Smallpox, ulcers, maggots, flies, filth—you're working in it all the time! Haven't you thought of the danger?"

Frances fresh from a shower, struggled through a clean white slip.

"Of course, I've thought of the danger," she said as soon as her head came through the top. "What nurse wouldn't hesitate to get into that mess out there on the hill? And if I were in it alone I would never climb up there, never help those horrible cases, never dare to get so close to lice and rats and flies. But 'Stasia, the Sisters are doing it. This may sound crazy to you— so long as I am with God's servants, I am sure no harm will come to me."

FRIDAY, APRIL 6. *Many more patients at the Clinic this morning. Frances Register, the Army Lieutenant of the Nursing Corps, now considers this her second home. She frequently comes to help us in off-duty hours. This afternoon she went with Sister Augusta to Yong Do, a section of huts up on the hill behind us where they vaccinated sixty children.*

We have found a number of smallpox cases. The best thing to do then is to gather the youngsters who live in the shacks around the spot, and vaccinate them. That's how Sister Augusta met Rhin Doh.

Rhin is a ten-year-old with a penchant for hanging around the American soldiers. He and two of his friends met Sister Augusta toiling up the hill and followed her, showing off the English they knew. It was pretty awful; swear words popped up every other word. Sister doesn't know enough Korean to tell him that he was not exactly giving forth gems of lyric English. So she held him firmly by the arm until Sister Mercy caught up with them.

"It's English all right," Sister Mercy explained to the lad, "but not the kind that good people use."

Ashamed, Rhin ran away from all this theology. But in a few minutes he was back with his two friends who had fled from the scene.

"Can we help you?" they said. Fatal words to say to a missioner! It's an invitation to an unending job. But the three lads seem to like it, for they've come to help Sister Augusta every time she is vaccinating in the vicinity. She brought three lollypops for them, some the G.I.'s gave us. She handed them to the boys out in the street. It was a mistake of course. In a matter of seconds a mob of little ones was around her screaming for food. They are so hungry! Of course she had none to give them. Then she saw Rhin and his pals beating and pounding their lollypops to break off pieces for the late comers. That's what we mean when we say these Koreans share their nothing.

SUNDAY, APRIL 8. Sister Agnus Therese came back from her trip to Mat Shed Hill, as we call the refugee colony up the mountainside back of us. She has seen her typhoid-pneumonia-asthma patient up there again along with some twenty or twenty-five others. Sister is discouraged about the girl. "She had a gastric hemorrhage today," she said. "She surely will die if I can't get chloromycetin for her." Somewhere in our meager store of medicines, we found just half the recommended dose. It is all we have; prayers will have to make it do the work of a full dose.

Even though it is raining again, Sister Agnus Therese went back up the hill with the chloromycetin.

MONDAY, APRIL 9. *The girl is some better but still very sick.*

TUESDAY, APRIL 10. *Sister Agnus Therese and Sister Caritas (a Korean Sister who goes along as interpreter and aide) came home today with beaming faces. The girl's temperature is normal and chest complications are clearing up.*

"I'll never forget it!" exulted Sister Agnus Therese. "I took the thermometer out of her mouth and it registered normal. We all cried—the girl's mother, the patient, Sister Caritas and I. What a good cry we had!"

Thank God for chloromycetin! It is completely unavailable here and of course very expensive even in the States. We pray that some will come our way before another such patient comes under our care.

WEDNESDAY, APRIL 18. *Mat Shed Hill is a honeycomb of all the things we would love to see corrected. Every day we find new and serious cases. Min Go is two years old and just a skeleton covered with skin. She will soon go to heaven with tuberculous meningitis, just a terribly tragic little girl for whom we can do nothing now. Her sister, Nung Go, just four, met us yesterday with a sore arm. She could not sleep the night before and the slightest movement of the arm is painful. We hope to be able to get someone in the UN setup to take an X-ray, for it probably is a tuberculous destructive process with a fracture at the elbow.*

Last Monday we vaccinated fifty youngsters out there because a full-blown smallpox case was found in one of the sheds. The next day we vaccinated sixty more. We set up a table and chair out in the open, round up the children and give it to them with no more ado except keeping a record of those vaccinated. Just as we finished we spied another case of smallpox—a baby on its mother's back, its small face a mass of crusty pustulas.

Last week at the Clinic here, a little boy of five died of beri-beri—pure malnutrition—starved to death. He was too far gone to save by the time we saw him. We are fighting what may be a losing battle for a little girl with the same condition.

Sister Agnus Therese writes to her mother:

April 26, 1951

Dearest Mother,

Days here are very busy. We see one hundred or so patients in the clinic in the morning and usually spend the afternoon hiking up and down the mountains to visit those too sick to come.

This week our little Ming Go, a two-year-old with TB meningitis, died. Also the little girl with whooping cough and beriberi whom we tried so desperately to save. These dear people are so undernourished that any disease catches them without a fighting chance.

However, my typhoid-pneumonia-asthma patient is steadily improving. Also a new meningitis which we caught early is responding well to penicillin and sulfa.

There is quite a bit of smallpox around. A few days ago Sister Caritas and I set out to do some vaccinating where we had seen cases. Arriving at what might be called a street corner up there on Mat Shed Hill, we quickly drew a crowd and asked how many children had ever been vaccinated. Almost none. So we looked about for a spot to set up business.

"Use my shop, honorable Su Nyo," said a very sweet woman who had a tiny rice store there on the corner.

"You will be swamped with youngsters if we do," I told her. "But we will use the space outside the shop if you don't mind."

The only trouble was that it was quite narrow. We often nearly fell into a four-foot ditch at the edge.

In no time at all about 140 youngsters were vaccinated. We then went around to the nearby shacks and saw about forty people too sick to stir out of their sheds. Most were

34

children. *Anybody needing more complete examination was referred to the Clinic.*

Then we packed up our tools and set out to walk another mile to Yong Do. As you know, Pusan is all mountains. We pass over one of the highest on the way to Yong Do. High at the top we paused a moment to eat our picnic lunch. The scenery was glorious. The eye takes in the entire harbor and wanders out over the deep blue sea to Japan. Fukuoka is only sixty miles away; it seemed today that we could almost see it.

Among the patients at Yong Do was a baby who had been bitten by a centipede. This is really dangerous; the centipede's bite is as poisonous as a snake's. It is impossible to keep the shacks free of crawling things. The best we can do is to pray that centipedes and such-like find better things to bite than innocent little babies.

We saw a number of other patients, all of them lying on makeshift beds of folded clothes or ancient straw mats or cardboard cartons flattened out—anything to keep the dampness out, for the floors are only the bare ground covered at best with sacks. Finally we wended our way home. The walking is wonderful and I surely love it, especially when my little Korean Sister Caritas comes along. We talk Korean all day long. No one could imagine—not even you, Mother dear— how I love these people. I have only one fear—that the Communists may drive us away.

Yesterday we had a half free day. Like busmen on a holiday we visited one of the American Station Hospitals here. Some of the nurses come to see us frequently and had given us a warm invitation. It is a former school. (I believe I told you that classes now are held all over the Pusan hillsides.)

Colonel Zalhan, chief of surgery, took us through. Such work! They do about one hundred operations per twenty-four hours, working on twelve-hour shifts. Rightly proud they are of the fact that theirs is the lowest mortality rate in military history.

35

The wounded boys are flown or brought by train to Pusan and transferred by ambulance to the hospital. Admitted to a pre-operative ward, they are immediately evaluated as to condition and work to be done. After surgery they are sent to another ward and if not in serious condition transferred to Japan within twenty-four hours. You can imagine the turnover. More than 50,000 soldiers have passed through this hospital in the last nine months.

Colonel Zalhan is an orthopedic surgeon, which is wonderful; nearly all war injuries involve bone. They have an excellent laboratory and all the necessities of modern American medicine in spite of the adverse physical circumstances.

I only wish I had the time to write to everyone about my beloved Korea, but time just isn't. Every spare moment is with the people or studying the language. 'Bye now.

APRIL 21. Best news yet! Today's plane brought some of the medicines we cabled for. National Catholic Welfare Council has acted promptly. This is a token shipment worth $500. If it were more, an export license would be needed, Father Wycislo explained. So he sent this much for the present emergency without waiting for a license. When they get the license the rest of the shipment will come.

Many Army and Navy doctors and nurses and other hospital personnel are taking an interest in our work. They give us financial help as well as supplies and we have received some exceptionally fine gifts of medicine—penicillin, streptomycin, etc. Today we were given an offer of blood for transfusion any time we need it. Outdated blood cannot be used by the Army, though technically it would be safe to use for another week or two. We received blood that was just outdated and never had an unfavorable reaction.

God has blessed our care of some very ill patients. Consequently, the people turn to us and beg us to come to see their sick. Several children who could not walk a few weeks ago are

36

playing on the hillside with their friends beacuse we were able to help them with injections of Vitamin B. (We have come to the last bottle now.)

Water is scarce and contaminated. The children are emaciated and many suffer acutely from vitamin deficiencies and lack of food. All the children in one of the refugee areas have whooping cough. We are trying to control whooping-cough epidemics in several other localities, too.

There are several other clinics here in Pusan operated by a number of agencies. They are no doubt all overcrowded and unable to do more than take care of the lines which come up for treatment there. We are the only ones going to the people in their homes where so much misery and suffering are hidden. These poor sick are too ill to go to a clinic and too timid usually to ask an M.D. to come to see them. Most of them do not have enough to eat; much less would they be able to pay for medicines. Every patient I have seen in his home is seriously ill. He would not be cared for if we did not go to him. There seem to be no minor complaints; everything is serious.

Sister Mercy writes home:

April 26, 1951

Any trip to visit a patient at his home turns out to be an afternoon clinic on the mountainside. The people are the poorest of the poor, protected from rain or sunshine by shacks made of cartons and old rice sacks. All their cooking utensils seem to be old tin cans.

We crawl into these homes on hands and knees. Usually there is room for only one of us to enter. Once in, we must kneel or sit since we are too tall to stand. Several times, I have crawled into such a place to find pus-filled pocks on a baby's face—full-blown smallpox—or to meet the luminous eyes of a fever-racked typhus case.

Then the immunization program begins! Sometimes we

set up our vaccination table out in the open; sometimes we are offered one of the matsheds. In any event, some of the boys of the neighborhood always come to our rescue, rounding up people to be vaccinated, writing down the data, etc. Everywhere I go I find forty or fifty patients to be examined and a hundred or more vaccinations to be done. The people are most grateful and are so happy to have us come to them in their poor homes. But their greatest joy is that we can speak to them in Korean.

APRIL 30. End of the first month! Word is spreading around to refugees that American nuns are taking care of them. Crowds are coming to the Clinic, small as it is. Today we hit a new high in numbers—320 patients this morning.

We end the month with five of us here in Korea, a medical team of two doctors, Sister Mercy and Sister Agnus Therese; a nurse, Sister Augusta; the business woman of us all, Sister André, and Sister Rose of Lima who is a pharmacist as well as a nurse. This makes her two people, but, unfortunately, she has only twenty-four hours to work in each day just like us single people. We could never take care of everybody were it not for the Korean Sisters who are helping out so beautifully.

Results for the month as tallied up:

2,212 patients were treated at the Clinic.

535 sick calls were made to homes.

Oh yes, and the Baby Clinic is going up—literally. It will be a special pediatric clinic built on the grounds but apart from the adult clinic. This should save time for poor women who must stand hours in line holding their sick children until their turn comes.

4

Chloromycetin and Flat Feet

*Oh no, 'twas the Truth in her eyes ever shining
That made me love Mary, the Rose of Tralee.*

Nice song. Nice voice! Sister Rose of Lima, away back in her girlhood days in Jersey City, had ideas of doing something with that voice. Her music teacher had plans, too. Her voice was fine, her face photogenic, her poise gracious and yet dignified.

But all those ideas flew out the window when Ann Robinson thought of God unknown and unloved by millions He had made and redeemed. She went in for pharmacy, taking a degree at Fordham, and later became a nurse as well.

And here she was in a sweltering hot shack built up against a clinic in war-torn Korea, singing "The Rose of Tralee" as she prepared medicines for the three hundred or so patients expected during the day. Happy as a lark, and tuneful as one, too.

Little Sister Caritas, Korean Sister of Perpetual Help, was folding up newspaper squares into small packets. She dropped two pills in each and folded it over. She smiled in her quiet way as she stacked the packets in a cigar box labelled IONIAZID DOSES.

"Some day, I teach you our national hymn," she said. "Sounds good, American singing that!"

Sister Rose of Lima stopped half-way in the process of pouring tincture of belladona into a big jar of phenobarbital.

"Look!" she pointed out the window. "Aren't they pathetic?"

39

"They" were an old man and an old woman. Between them was a child with matted hair, and lack-luster eyes set in a face and body so swollen it was grotesque. They were sitting in their rags on the ground, very apathetic, not seeming to care whether they lost their place in the line. Just then the people behind, annoyed at their not moving forward, stepped around them and closed in the gap ahead. The old couple and the child hardly looked up.

"In Pusan these days you're pretty far gone when you don't care about that," decided Sister Rose of Lima. "Let's get them!"

It took persuasive talk to get behind the blankness, but at last the old couple struggled to their feet. Grandpa was almost bent over double as he toddled along. Sister Caritas carried the child; Sister Rose of Lima led the way with Grandma leaning heavily on her. They came through the back gate and over to the shed which served as kitchen. Seated on boxes backed up against the wooden wall, the old couple closed their eyes and groaned after the exertion.

Then came bowls of hot milk and buns. The grimy old hands reached out eagerly. The child had to be fed. Hot soup followed. A smile, a word of thanks, Grandpa got up and bowed politely. Grandma found the energy to take over feeding the child, holding the bowl up to her mouth and tilting it gently.

Ah, the climax—hot baths! They seem to be refined people! How they must have hated to be so dirty and full of lice! But water costs twenty-five hwaun for a small pail. When you don't have the hwaun you simply go dirty. That's all there is to it.

Sister Rose of Lima had to run back and forth to the pharmacy to keep things going there, but she was on hand for each stage of the reclamation. When the new clothes were put on, that was the cherry on top of the whipped cream. Grandpa walked almost as straight as an arrow. Wonderful what clothes do for a man! In khaki trousers and shirt he looked like Captain Daredevil of the Do-or-Die Legion. Really a handsome old fellow! Grandma was beautiful in a new white muslin Korean dress, smiling and bowing. Her sloe-eyes danced!

40

Ah Kim, the child, didn't do so well. She was swollen and weak from malnutrition. It would take many a bowl of hot milk and many a bun to put her into good condition, if she made the grade at all.

Sister Rose of Lima and Sister Caritas watched them off down the street, toting little Ah Kim between them. Grandpa had an armful of food which should keep them for a few days. With new clothes, his hopes of getting a job were soaring. There was a bounce in Grandma's Korean shoes. She was planning breakfast, dinner and supper; and breakfast, dinner and supper after that. Two days of food ahead! Surely God was good!

MAY 2. *Of all the destitute and pitiful cases that have come to us, today's was perhaps the worst. The patients waiting in line—a line, by the way, that extends for a block down the street and around the corner—told Sister André about her. Sister was Admission Clerk at the time, making out cards for each patient so that in the future we can refer to the case without getting confused. Korean names are terrific. Anybody not a Kim must be a Chang, or a Rhee. We have to resort to numbers as the main identification factor.*

The patients in line called out to Sister André, "She's crawling, Su Nyo. She's exhausted. Take her first." True enough. The woman had crawled on her hands and knees a distance that would take a well person an hour and a half to walk. Four or five miles, I would say. She had been here once before, several weeks ago. She had used all the medicine we gave her and made up her mind to return for more. We treated her and gave her some food and rest. Then, as some soldiers were here visiting, we prevailed upon them to take her home by jeep.

Sister Agnus Therese writes to her mother:

May 3, 1951

My days are packed full to the brim. I am so happy to be practicing medicine here where there is so much need, to

41

bring joy and love to lives so filled with trouble and grief. Let me describe yesterday to you. It will give you an idea of how my days go.

We rise at 5:20 and have Mass and prayers in our chapel. Then breakfast. I make my bed and hurry to a Korean lesson with Sister Caritas, one of the Korean Sisters living here. The weather is warm now, so we go outside—just one of many classes perched on any convenient spot on our grounds! At 9:30 I change to my cotton habit and the day's work begins. I wear a cotton habit on these trips. The streets and alleyways are so dirty, and I have to get into such tight quarters with sick people that a woolen habit would be very impractical.

Yesterday morning after the Korean class a woman was waiting for me.

"My husband is sick," she said. "Please, you come with me."

As we walked uphill, the woman (whose name was Cecilia) apologized for taking us to her tiny home. Climbing partway up the mountain covered with matshed one-room huts, we paused before a hole in the hill.

"This is our home," Cecilia said.

I took off my shoes and dropped to my hands and knees, crawling through the hole after her. As my eyes became adjusted to the darkness, I found myself crawling down an incline which dropped about three feet into the room. This was about five feet by four feet and not high enough to stand up in. Lying in this damp cave, like a sick rabbit dying in his burrow, was a man of about thirty. His face was flushed but he managed to smile a welcome. Fever was 104.2. On raising his shirt I saw the telltale typical rash of typhus. Fortunately, we had some aureomycin and I began him on it immediately. Despite this, he was wildly delirious when I returned this morning. Chloromycetin would have been much better, but we have none.

We have notified Public Health, but so far they have not

42

come to take him to the isolation hospital. Perhaps it is already full. After crawling back into the sunshine, we did our best to reassure Cecilia, urging her to call a priest if he should get worse, for they are Catholics.

From here, Sister Caritas and I went up to my "Hill." The Sisters jokingly call it that because this is where the typhus patient—my first in Korea—lives. I visited her so often that the Sisters think I own the place. Of course, I dropped in to see Mok Chang again. What a thrill; she walked across the room to greet me!

"Where's your mother?" I asked. Then came the sad story. The elderly woman had gone to work in the country for a few days. Either she stepped into something, or the unaccustomed manual work did it, but she has blistered and swollen hands and feet. She'd gone to our clinic this morning to get some relief.

Then we visited other patients round about. A young woman getting over pneumonia. A baby who a few days ago had about six convulsions from intestinal worms. A man of about thirty with three small children—he has had a fever of 103 with aching all over his body. Yesterday the rash began and the diagnosis was clinched—another typhus. He, too, is on aureomycin but not responding as I would like him to. Oh, for some chloromycetin! As soon as we finished with him, an excited woman pulled us into the shack next door to see her husband. I suspect typhus with him, too.

Small wonder! These people are not inoculated, and with sanitary conditions as they are in these refugee camps, lice are prevalent. Now, Mother, don't worry about me! All of us are well inoculated and get booster shots every month or so. The poor people must buy water and then carry it long distances up steep inclines. Of course it is very precious and is used sparingly for baths. It is well nigh impossible to keep these tiny sheds free from crawling things. We are trying to get DDT from the Army to dust all these people and their

43

bedding. *Because these conditions are such a danger to UN personnel, we will probably be able to get it.*

From this shed where the typhus suspect lives, we crossed the ridge of the mountain to another refugee area on the other side. Here we saw a dear old grandmother. I expected to hear that she had died, but she lives on. For years this old lady had been plagued with families of worms in her interior. About a week ago, she decided to take enough medicine to get rid of them once and for all. But she took too much and had a kidney shutdown with resulting uremia. The day before yesterday she was unconscious and twitching. Her limbs were cold and she breathed strangely. She was unconscious today, too, and probably will not pull through in spite of our best efforts. Her dear old husband and son and daughter-in-law are so grateful! Yet the joy is all mine to have anything to give them.

Close to this house a crowd clustered around another shack. I had been visiting a young woman dying of TB in this place.

"Very very serious, Su Nyo," the crowd warned me. "You had better not go in."

Leaning up against the closed door was Syun Go, the patient's little eight-year-old daughter, with the year-old baby tied on her back. She was sobbing; even the tiny one seemed to sense the tragedy going on inside that house. Removing our shoes—for no one enters even the poorest hovel in Korea without taking off his shoes—we pushed back the door and stooped to pass under the low lintel. Too late! Our patient had already taken her last breath. She had died all alone. These people are so afraid of tuberculosis that no one had the courage to stay with her.

Knowing that she had expressed a desire to be baptized and had just drawn her last breath, we baptized her conditionally. Then Sister and I lifted her body onto the mat and covered her. The neighbors looked on from the doorway. They

44

were amazed that I was not afraid to touch the dead. Here, the custom is to dress the dying in the clothes they are to be buried in so that they need not be touched after death.

This dear woman's husband was hurrying home from the market. He had not arrived before we had to leave. Syun Go wanted to see her mother again, so I held the baby while she went into the room alone and stayed a few minutes. As she came out to the sunshine again she seemed to have grown up in those few moments. She was the little mother now at eight years of age. She took the baby from me and tied him to her back with the customary sash. Then she set about straightening out the things about the charcoal fire. These are the kind of scenes which bind one's heart to Korea with ties which can never be broken.

After this call we went home for dinner at noon.

Yong Do in the afternoon. Here we vaccinated 108 children for smallpox. I saw thirty-five patients sick with everything imaginable, beriberi, diarrhoea, pneumonia, TB, pink eye, epilepsy, cardiac failure, typhoid and worms. The biggest thrill was to have my beriberi patient up and around. Due to severe malnutrition she had not walked for more than two months since the birth of the baby. Even the infant, Paul, is beginning to fill in the hollows in his cheeks and to cover the bony angles with a bit of padding.

So we were very hungry and happy when we got home about 7:30 for supper, prayers and recreation.

You would laugh at our bathing system. We have pitchers and basins for washing—really old fashioned. Each evening, the cook leaves a big rice-pot of water on the dying embers to heat. Then at bedtime (9:00 P.M.) we each take a pitcher and ladle out hot water for a bath. We have to walk across an open court from the kitchen to our dormitory so the water loses some of its heat en route. But it is very comforting to have clean hot water to use.

I know you are collecting medicines to send me, Mother.

45

Sister Mercy has gotten two packages already by air express, one from New York and one from Milwaukee. You can send yours the same way; I am sure it will come all right. I cannot thank you and Dad enough. It means the difference between life and death to these poor people who have no energy left to fight disease. How I wish you and Dad could see the gratitude of these people you are saving with the "miracle drugs." And as you collect more, remember—

Chloromycetin will be most welcome!

It was late. Sister Mercy knew right well she ought to be in bed. She was afraid to look at her watch. Just one more letter, and then I'll go to bed, she promised herself; common sense was just then prodding her unmercifully.

With one hand up against her forehead, she shaded her eyes from the glare of the single electric bulb hanging over her desk, a former packing box. She was afraid lest the light would glint through the cracks in the bare wooden partition and disturb the other Sisters in the dormitory. "I must get something to make this little cubby-hole lightproof," she thought, and bent over her paper.

"*Dear John,*" she began to her brother, John Hirschboeck, Dean of Marquette's Medical College in Milwaukee. "*Conditions are pretty bad here,*" she wrote, making, perhaps The Understatement of the Year. "*You are in touch with other doctors and pharmaceutical houses, and you may be able to help us. The people suffer badly from vitamin deficiencies. Tetanus and whooping cough are prevalent, too. See what you can do to get chloromycetin, penicillin and other antibiotics. NCWC sent us some but we are running out of everything. Patients are around three hundred a day here. We have taken a tiny hut on the mountainside for an auxiliary clinic. It is made of rice straw and burlap but serves us well enough for now.*

Here at the main Clinic we have added a pediatrics treat-

46

ment room. The dispensary floor is made of boards from packing boxes. Thank God we had enough shipping crates to supply wood for most of the floor. We will now try to get some furniture and outfit the place to care for the thousands of needy children right around us."

MAY 12.   *The medicines came! NCWC's large shipment arrived today. We are glorying in the selection. Some 9,000 doses of tetanus antitoxin; 2,500 vials of pertussin vaccine against whooping cough and 5,000 capsules of chloromycetin. This last alone will save many lives up on Sister Agnus Therese's hill. She couldn't wait to finish the unpacking, but tucked some of the precious stuff into her bag and was off up there to give it to her special-specials—those who need it most.*

Sister Mercy hopes that this medicine will break the back of the cruel whooping cough epidemic now devastating the refugee areas. Whooping cough has frequent complications of pneumonia in malnourished children. It's so much more serious here than in the States.

Monsignor Carroll is now asking NCWC to send us food and clothing as well. He is representative for NCWC War Relief Services, and in charge of distribution of supplies sent by American Catholics at home.

Mignon Johnson, Navy nurse from the hospital ship *Repose*, paused with her paintbrush in her hand. She had been on the point of applying the first brushful of white enamel to a table made of packing box boards when a thought struck her. It was all well and good that she and other Army and Navy nurses spent their free moments helping the Sisters at this dispensary, but in the States there was a vast potential of help which was untapped.

Nurse Johnson surveyed the room. Destined to be a pediatrics clinic, it was fairly large and sturdy. She and Captain Little and Lt. Donovan had spent many an off-duty hour making examining tables, treatment chairs and partitions, and painting them white.

Outside, she could hear some G.I.'s constructing a covered waiting room so that patients would not have to stand in broiling sun or pelting rain.

Through the doorway into the main Clinic she watched Sister Mercy. It was five in the afternoon, already. Sister Mercy had been working since eight that morning, examining, recording, checking, treating one poor soul after another. Dysentery, worms, T.B., whooping cough, relapsing fever! Over in a corner, a woman was huddled in a shabby man's overcoat, her feet wrapped in a blanket. And yet she shivered on this mild May day. This was malaria. In a few minutes she would be burning in fever.

Five o'clock! Outside, the line was as long as ever. Mignon Johnson knew from experience that Sister Mercy would be working at 8 P.M. Sister Augusta would be giving injections to babies in another room; Sister Rose of Lima making prescriptions in the pharmacy cubicle; Sister André checking admission cards at the entrance, carefully sorting out the Kims and the Rhees and the Changs and sending them to the proper places for treatment. And Sister Agnus Therese was out in the hills, visiting the sick in their shacks, vaccinating children in the noisome alleyways. She might be back by 7:30 for supper—or might not.

Others would keep on working, too—Dr. Rhee, the Korean medical man, who never stopped to think of his own comfort; Nita, the faithful nurse, and Agada; Christina, too, and the Korean Sisters of Perpetual Help. The Navy nurses who came in off-duty hours would be busy turning their hands to any job from giving injections to, like herself, painting furniture. Mignon could see Frances Register, the Army nurse, now acting as medical secretary for Sister Mercy.

"This is going to grow and grow," Nurse Johnson said to herself. "They're going to need more and more medicines, clothes, food. Those of us here in Korea who see it with our own eyes, will be doing whatever we can—carpenters, elec-

48

tricians, general handymen, as well as the medically trained servicemen and women.

"But folks at home will want to cash in spiritually, so to speak, on this operation. They can get supplies for us. I'll start with my own friends and relatives."

That settled, she brought down the brushful of paint on the table. In half an hour she'd finished the last table for the new pediatrics clinic, due to open its doors on the morrow, and jogged back to the hospital ship to write a lot of letters home to Chicago.

> *"The dispensary, you might say, is made from packing boxes, even to the floor. But you would be amazed how well it looks. The new room will be in use tomorrow. Instead of seeing three hundred patients a day, they will be seeing six hundred a day in the dispensary, besides making many, many home calls. The vast amount of work the Sisters have undertaken here is amazing, even frightening. I am concerned, as all of them have lost weight but will not spare themselves. Their dispositions are just as cheery. They never complain. What really kills me is that they are so appreciative for the help we give them even though it isn't much. Sister Mercy told me the other day, 'There is so much to be done and we consider it a real privilege to be here.' Can you imagine that, when those of us in the Service are counting the days until we get home!*
>
> *"I have been with the Sisters long enough to know that God is looking after them. Everytime the cupboard is bare, some help comes. Nonetheless, I'm writing to you all to make sure that it keeps coming. Maryknoll and NCWC War Relief Services are sending things, but it takes a mighty long time for anything to reach us."*

Sister Agnus Therese writes to her mother:

Thank God for flat feet! I have adopted Korean shoes. One can slip in and out of them so easily, don't have to bend over to untie shoe laces when entering the homes. No one wears shoes in a Korean house, even if it is only a hole in the side of a hill. A good idea, if you ask me, not to have mud or dust tracked into the house. So I'm grateful to God for my flat feet; I'm perfectly comfortable without heels or arch supports.

The Clinic is growing by leaps and bounds. We took care of 350 yesterday in both the adult and pediatric work. I begin the pediatrics clinic at 9:00 A.M. and keep going steadily until 1:00 P.M. or often later. To make best use of the time, we have two examining cubicles and I go from one to the other. A nurse undresses the little ones and takes the temperature first. So many are so pitifully thin and so very sick.

Yesterday I had a little boy of five with T.B. meningitis. He had been diagnosed by spinal tap at a Korean hospital and received four days of streptomycin. The family had no more money so they took the child home then. He grew worse, of course. After ten days someone told them of our Clinic. Knowing he needs hospital care, I was able to get him in at the Korean Children's Hospital. This was started by American G.I. doctors in their time off, several months ago. It is a wonderful tribute to the American boys' love and solicitude for children. They have about seventy patients, and over a hundred well orphans in an adjoining building.

The doctors work all day at their Army stations and then at night at the hospital. They keep these youngsters fed, clothed and medicated.

Oh, I started out to tell you about my Korean shoes. Today, I'm showing off a new pair given me by some good Korean fairy godmother. As I left a miserable home yesterday, I glanced along the row of Korean shoes beside the door, looking for the special lining I keep in mine, a bright red leather to soften the stones on the roads. I found the pair I was looking for and stepped into them.

Only when I was entering the next home did I notice that the shoes were brown, not black. Still the lining, I am sure, is mine. The only solution is that the family I was visiting last must have noticed the soles coming off the old shoes. They got these for me and unobtrusively left them outside with my own lining.

They may have been embarrassed to present them outright. My feet, you know, are huge for a woman. My size comes only in the styles for men!

Mother dear, can you do me another favor? The Korean Sisters of Our Lady of Perpetual Help support themselves mostly by embroidery work. They have great difficulty getting good embroidery cotton. They can get linen for towels, luncheon sets, etc., which the boys love to send home as souvenirs of Korea—but dye-fast thread, just doesn't grow in Japan. Can you send some D.C. embroidery cotton in all colors, especially the pastel shades? Send it air mail. Thank you, Mother, already; I know you will be happy to help them.

5

Pyong Il Takes to the Beer Can

It was June. Beginning to get hot and stuffy. Colonel Laurence P. Devlin of the Medical Corps did not mind too much, however. He was glad to be in Pusan for a few days away from the front lines where the business was killing. It was his first time in the city.

He stepped smartly from his quarters to the waiting jeep. The driver saluted and they got in.

"To headquarters, Tom," Colonel Devlin said and they left the neat Army enclosure with its well laid out plots of grass, its white-washed barracks, its general air of orderly well-being.

The jeep edged out into the street, tried to make a way through the crowds who overflowed the sidewalks into the main street.

"Awfully crowded, isn't it!" remarked the Colonel.

"Yes, Sir," Tom agreed. "This little old town used to have 250,000 people in it. There's close to a million now, they say."

The Colonel looked about him. People flocked the streets walking and milling aimlessly around. The stench from the gutter was almost unbearable; quite a few men, women and children were using them as toilets. Children were even toddling around in the filth.

"Rather early for all these people to be out, isn't it?" the Colonel asked.

"Oh, they walk around like this all night, too, Sir," said Tom. "They haven't any place to go."

The Colonel's brows drew together in pity, but he didn't know what he could do about it. His eye lighted on a woman lying on the street with her baby strapped to her back.

"Poor soul!" he thought. "She has to sleep in the street with the baby tied to her so that it won't wander away. She must be exhausted to stay asleep in all this clamor. Probably walked two or three hundred miles to safety. No wonder nothing can wake her now."

Later in the morning the Colonel was driving down the same street, with Tom again at the wheel. His conference at headquarters was over and he was looking forward to his few days in Pusan as a relief from gruelling work at the Front.

"There's that woman again!" he exclaimed. "Lying just as she was before, too. And the baby is screaming. It's a wonder that doesn't wake her up."

Tom turned his head to look straight at the Colonel.

"She's probably dead, Sir," he said quietly.

"Dead? Well, let's stop, for Heaven's sake."

They walked back to the spot. Sure enough, she had died. With thousands walking by, no one stopped, inquired, touched or cared about her.

"Is this common here in Pusan?" the Colonel asked his driver.

"I've been here several months, Sir," the boy replied. "I've seen a number of cases like this. All of us servicemen have."

"What does a person do?"

"Oh, nothing. Nobody does anything, Sir. We can't. There are too many. She'll be taken away tonight. The street cleaners . . . Well, they have a cart and they remove things like this."

The Colonel pulled out his handkerchief and covered the corpse's face. He stood up.

"What about the child?" he said at last. "Surely there is some agency which will take care of it."

Tom spread his hands. "I don't know of any agency in town,

53

Sir. But I think the Maryknoll Sisters up on Tae Chong Dong Road might be able to find somebody to care for it."

"Lead the way, Tom," the Colonel said, stooping to untie the howling baby from its dead mother. "We're going to see those Sisters."

Late that night the Colonel was writing to all his friends in Philadelphia.

"I want to tell you what these five Maryknoll Sisters are doing here in Pusan under the direction of Sister Mary Mercy, who is a physician. There is another Sister, a convert to Catholicism (from Philadelphia, by the way) who is also an M.D. Then there is a Sister pharmacist and two nurses.

"These truly heroic Sisters have moved into a house here in Pusan and have opened a clinic to treat the sick and destitute. They work from morning to night without taking sufficient time, in my opinion, for meals, rest and relaxation.

"Between four and five hundred people are treated every day. The Sisters also provide, from their own meager stores of food, sustenance for the poor Korean Carmelite nuns who were tossed out of Seoul convent by the Communists. The Reds abducted other Sisters, too, and Bishop Byrne, and nothing has been heard from them. It is all part of the Commie plan to exterminate Christianity, for the Church has been making headway in Korea and the present Catholic population is about 350,000 in South Korea.

"What I want you to do is. . . ."

Another group of helpers in the States began getting money and supplies for Korean refugees.

Sister André lay in her bed wide awake. Ten o'clock! She should be asleep if she were ever to face that 5:15 A.M. bell with any spiritual fortitude.

To say the truth, her legs ached. Walk, walk, walk. All day long she had been walking. Upstairs to get supplies. Down to the pier to see about unloading a shipment. Over to the customs office for the proper forms. Then back home to tell the Army lads just where the new waiting room was to be. Up the hill to the cloistered Carmelite Sisters to give them some of the food packages which had just been bought. Stopping by at the kitchen to see if everything was going right there. Supervising the laborers who were laying new water pipes to the children's clinic. Yes, her legs ached and her heart ached, too.

"There are four hundred out there tonight," she said to herself. "They have brought their sleeping mats if they have them, and are prepared to stay the night so as to hold a place in line for tomorrow. Sick people! And they have waited in line from five o'clock this afternoon!"

The low murmur of the crowd out in the street floated up to her ears. There were hawkers out selling bread sticks, and rice cakes, and dubious messes to pour over rice. Now and then a subdued squabble rose, flourished stridently for a moment or two, and then was sh-h-h-h-h-h-d down to silence again. Often a baby's cry wailed above the general stirring, wobbled as the mother vigorously shook the baby on her back, and lapsed once more into the crowd's murmur.

On the whole, they were very quiet for being so many. Part of it was for their own comfort. They were trying to get as much sleep as they could on the street. But part was also consideration for the Sisters. "Hush! The Sisters are sleeping!" came up to Sister André's window as a self-constituted policeman put down another minor ruckus.

"More than six hundred passed through the clinic today." Sister André's last conscious thought for the day was business like. "Please, dear God, let us help that many and more tomorrow."

"Of all the slippery mud I have waddled through in my mission travels," Sister Mercy typed under the lone electric bulb hanging from the ceiling of her tiny office, "Pusan clay is the slipperiest of all.

55

"I had a call to the highest point on the highest mountain in town today. Well, you should have seen me!

"The mother of the patient (a young man with T.B.) said she was so sorry that the Sister-doctor who is so old (I like that —at forty-eight!) was having such trouble puffing up the hill. There were some perilous spots. The path is very narrow and overhangs a precipice. One of my companions would pull and the other push, both clutching my habit so that I would not fall.

"I have waddled through mud in my days in Bolivia, but Pusan's is tops. I lost my footing more than once. Soon I was coated with it but we kept going up and up. Occasionally down, too!

"With all this we had a great following. People on this mountainside had never seen a Sister before, and my speaking Korean intrigued them. They are used to Americans now, but not to Americans who speak their language.

"I was amused at hearing all the remarks about my age as I went along. It impressed everyone that an old lady should climb this terrible mountain to see a poor sick boy. My special patient at the top of the mountain was a man of twenty-two, dying of tuberculosis. His disposition was fine and we instructed and baptized him.

"Many of the bystanders wanted to know about the Church. The fact that I spoke Korean and also that I puffed my way up the hill made them wonder why I did it."

Sergeant Snow L. Wilson, feature writer for *Pacific Stars and Stripes*, the Army newspaper, sauntered into the pre-fab building which served as Pusan's editorial office. It was early July, hot, sticky, dusty.

"My nose for news is out of joint, Bill," he told the city-editor. "I can't seem to smell out any good stories here in Pusan. Orphanage stories, girl-show stories, features of boys in the hospitals, brave-men stories—I'm tired of them all."

"Ever hear the story of the cub-reporter who was sent to

56

cover a society wedding?" asked the city-editor, leaning back in his swivel chair and bracing his feet on the desk.

"Can't say as I did. Shoot!" Sergeant Wilson upturned the wastebasket beside the desk and sat on it.

"Well, this fellow went out to cover the wedding and came back to the city-room all right. But he sat down sort of discouraged at his desk and didn't do anything.

" 'Come on! Get on with that wedding story,' yelled the city-editor. 'I'll be needing it soon.'

" 'There isn't any wedding story,' said the cub.

" 'What happened? Didn't you get there?' demanded the boss.

" 'Sure. I was there all right,' the young fellow said. 'Only there wasn't any wedding.'

" 'Why not?' shouted the old Man.

"The cub was annoyed. 'There isn't any story, I'm telling you. There wasn't any wedding. You see, the roof of the church fell in and killed the bride and groom at the altar.' "

Sgt. Wilson laughed. "Good enough!" he said.

Bill took his feet off the desk and straightened the swivel chair.

"I saw a big crowd of Koreans down on Tae Chong Dong Road this morning," he said casually. "Don't know what it's all about but you might see what that crowd's doing there."

"Sure thing! Always good to investigate a crowd," said Sergeant Wilson as he left the room.

Later, in *The Stars and Stripes*, he wrote:

"On a hill overlooking the 2nd Logistical Command's busy port of Pusan is the Maryknoll Sisters' Clinic, home of five American nuns—five who talked SCAP into letting them return to Korea. Green grassy slopes surround the two buildings on the compound and hundreds of blooming shrubs make the spot a literal Garden of Eden. A lily pond with a dainty little bridge rounds out the landscape and little walks wind between the shady trees.

57

"For soldiers who pass by, it is a little world completely away from the dirt and filth of refugee-crowded streets. But the Sisters rarely get to enjoy it. They are far too busy and their moments of relaxation come only long after dark. Even then they are too tired to enjoy the garden. Instead, they try to get as much sleep as possible; for them the next day begins at 5:15 A.M.

"Morning prayers, Mass and meditation. Breakfast, too, of course. Then the day's work begins.

"By eight o'clock each morning the courtyard of the Clinic is crammed with ragged Korean refugees. All morning long the Sisters work. Sister Mercy, Superior, cares for case after case of relapsing fever, festering sores and every ailment known in the Orient. After treatment, she gives the prescription to Sister Rose of Lima, the pharmacist, for filling and goes on to another patient.

"At the same time, Sister Agnus Therese has her hands full caring for the hundreds of children. She makes sure vaccinations and inoculations are given each one if serum is available, and she doesn't stop until they are all taken care of.

"Working with her is Sister Augusta who treats the cuts and bruises and gives injections of serum and the new 'wonder drugs.' The two must work fast to care for everybody. Sister Mercy takes over the pediatric work in the afternoon so that Sister Agnus Therese can go out visiting the hovels that serve as homes in Pusan. Luckily, a jeep was donated to the Sisters recently to help in making calls.

"Taking a Korean Sister with her, Sister Agnus Therese drives far around the steep Southern Mountain of Pusan. Then she leaves the jeep and climbs down tiny trails that would tax a mountain goat. These patients are too weak to come to the clinic. Crawling into the pitiful little shelters on hands and knees, the two Sisters never know what they will meet. They are prepared for anything. Sometimes a horrible case of pus-filled pocks on the face of a child greets them, or a woman out of her mind with hunger. Or it might be typhus or typhoid. And everywhere they meet dire, bleak, rock-bottom poverty. But though half crazy with pain, each of the patients seems to understand that here is his own particular 'angel.'

"By late afternoon, tired and dirty, sometimes crawling with lice brushed into their clothes, the two Sisters are dog-tired when they get back to the clinic. The day's work is still not done; medicine has to be prepared for the next day and baths taken, plus a triple dose of DDT powder.

"With such a tremendous number of patients, the medical supplies often run low, but they rarely are out. Always just at the crucial moment something comes in. At the present time UNCACK (United Nations Civil Assistance Committee in Korea) is providing some of the drugs, but much comes from the States in answer to their requests.

"Sometimes these requests are a little misunderstood. The result is some anxiety and occasionally a bit of humor.

"An example was the request for enough whooping cough serum to vaccinate 2,000 children. The sender packed up 2,000 bottles of vaccine. This was enough serum to inoculate all the children in Korea. On top of that, it had to be kept cold. An icebox simply had to be obtained.

"The Sisters scraped the bottom of their barrel for money, and along with help from some Army personnel, the icebox was brought in, filling up nearly a whole side of their small store-room.

"Now, no matter what a child has when he comes to the clinic, the first procedure is an inoculation for whooping cough, so the serum is serving a purpose. 'If we only had the time,' Sister Augusta says, 'we could wipe out whooping cough in Korea.' "

At sixty, Kim Il Sunie found himself alone in the world, owning only a scraggly beard, the wreck of a horsehair hat (his emblem of respectability), an indomitable cheerfulness—and a six weeks' old grandson. It was not a bad list of assets for a refugee. The cheerfulness, especially. He got along fairly well with that.

The baby, however, presented a problem. How Kim Il Sunie came by it was a sad story. Eight months before, he had been living with his daughter and her family on a farm some distance from Pusan. In the early terror of war, as the Reds pushed down from the North, his son-in-law figured out a plan.

"You go to Pusan with your father," he told his wife. "There you can get a house and be safe when the baby is born. I will follow with the children in a few weeks when I have things settled up here. Get a good house; we'll find it and join you."

But everything had gone wrong. There was no good house available. And in the welter of refugees, the husband had never found his wife. That is, if he had come to Pusan at all. She had never heard. Maybe they were all killed in the old house. Maybe they died en route. Who knows?

The baby, Pyong Il, was born in dire poverty. His mother gave him everything she had. After a few weeks she died and her body, denied even ordinary burial, was tearfully laid on the street corner to be collected with others during the night.

Il Sunie now valiantly faced the fact that he had a baby on his hands with no means of feeding it. For some weeks he traded his services as handyman to various women in return for a square meal for his grandson. Pyong Il was not thriving on it and let Il Sunie know vociferously that he did not approve of this haphazard schedule.

"You're silly to bother with us," a woman told him at last. "Take the little one to the *Su Nyo Nim's* clinic. Get some powdered milk there."

"Are you crazy, woman?" he retorted. "Powdered milk? Where would I get money for that stuff? Even when I was head teacher in our village school, we couldn't afford powdered milk."

"Now you *are* silly," she countered. "This is the real thing. They give you milk if you need it. Look at the Pak's over there in that cave. They get food regularly. So do I, sometimes."

60

Thus it was that around five o'clock one morning, Il Sunie tied his grandson to his back and limped up this hill and down that hill, along this street and around that corner, until he joined the crowd on Tae Chong Dong Road. It had already formed into a tight line.

He sat himself down at the end of the pediatrics line. Wearily he fanned himself with the battered old hat.

"What are you doing here?" queried the woman in front of him. "This line is for women with babies."

"Well, this baby doesn't have any woman. All he has is an old man. I'm sticking in this line."

By this time there were three or four women behind him. The conversation, once started, bubbled along merrily. The women admired Pyong Il, pinched his wan cheek, and gave his Grandpa valuable advice. Several looked with envy at Pyong Il's straight little legs and admired his lusty voice. Their own children were not so fortunate. The woman in front carried a boy of two encased in a heavy plaster cast. T.B. of the spine. The child was restless; some fleas had gotten under the cast and were making merry on the poor tot. Behind him was a distraught mother whose baby was dying. There was little doubt of it. When Sister Augusta came down the line at eight o'clock looking for critical cases, she took the baby and its mother out of line and sent them up front for immediate attention.

The others, tense in the hope that they, too, would be called out of line, relaxed when the prospects faded.

"You're an old man," said the woman in front, "to be left to care for a tiny baby."

"Yes, I'm old all right," Il Sunie smiled. "Next month I pass Han Gap (The Great Birthday, sixty-one). Oh, we had a grand celebration planned for it. My son-in-law gave the order to the coffin-maker for a really handsome casket. He was going to present it to me with a fine lining and all the trimmings.

"Ah, well," he resigned himself, " 'tisn't likely I'll be needing it right away, anyhow. We'll put off the celebration ten years or so. This young fellow and I will have one beautiful party, won't we?" and he joggled Pyong Il companionably.

"Where do you live, Grandpa?" called a voice from up the line.

"I have my palatial apartments in Yong Do," shouted Il Sunie in fine good humor. "When you drive up in your fine car to call on me, tell my butler that you met me here today."

"That I will, Grandpa. Thanks for the invitation," the woman called back laughing.

"That's a long way for you to come with the baby," said a sympathetic woman who had closed in behind him when the dying baby was taken ahead. "I notice that you limp, too."

"The little one needs the milk, doesn't he?" said Il Sunie. "As for limping, that's good for a baby. All you mothers ought to limp when you carry a child. Heh! Heh! Gets them used early to the ups and downs in life!"

The line was moving fast now. Soon Il Sunie found himself up a stairway and past a gateman. It was Johnnie Rhee, a scrappy little man who could settle a dispute fast. He would have made a good baseball umpire. He called the plays and let the chips (or pop-bottles) fall where they may. Johnnie Rhee disdained to notice disagreement with his decisions.

Once past the gateman, Il Sunie found himself before a white-robed woman with a white something-else on her head. She wanted to know the queerest things about Pyong Il. Name, age, sex, address—how can you give an address when you live in a tent-like affair of gunny sacks and cardboard cartons which the next gale will move several blocks away?

But out of it all he got a card with a number on it and a handsome piece of wood (it was really a tongue depressor) with a red number blazoned thereon. This was the golden ticket of admission for Pyong Il. He would be seen by the doctor and given what he needed.

The card, Il Sunie was warned, he was to keep forever and ever. It would identify him in the future. He would not have to go through the process of being registered again if he merely showed this magic card to the admission clerk. "Sounds good to me!" Il Sunie told the *Su Nyo*.

What happened then was a blur to the old man. He carried Il Pyong into a small cubicle where the little fellow was whisked out of his hands. Quick as a flash a nurse had undressed him— easy enough for he had not much of anything on—and taken his temperature. She made some marks on a card, handed it to a bewildered Il Sunie and was off into the next cubicle. "Give it to the doctor when she comes in," were her last instructions.

No sooner was she out than another white-robed lady with a white something-else on her head (just like the one at the door) walked briskly into the cubicle. She stared at the marks on the card. Then she went over to Pyong Il and felt all over him. "Not bad shape," she commented, as if relieved to find one fairly healthy child in the morning. "Some malnutrition, though. Hmmm, mother dead, I see. Well, we will give you the milk for the baby. But you will have to find some way of getting it into him."

"Don't worry about that, *Su Nyo Nim*," Il Sunie reassured her. "You give me the milk. I'll take care of the rest."

Three days later, Pyong Il and his Grandpa were around once more.

"I'm an old friend, now," he said flashing his readmission card before Johnnie Rhee at the gate. "Also a neighbor. I moved my tent right next to your place. Aren't you glad to see me?" Johnnie Rhee let him in without comment.

But once they had passed Johnnie turned and stared. Stared and laughed. A Miller Highlife beer can protruded from the old fellow's hip pocket topped with a coil of rubber tubing so long that it looped around the can, passed under Il Sunie's arm around his neck and ended up on his chest at a spot convenient for Pyong Il to reach as he lay in the old man's arms.

Il Sunie defended his system to Sister Rose of Lima (Sister Nosalina he called her, as did the other Koreans). "The baby

63

can chew on it as a pacifier. Then when it's time to feed him I just lift the can up high and turn it over, squeezing the tubing at the end to let just a few drops of milk go into his mouth at a time. It works perfectly."

"I have to admit it does," Sister "Nosalina" concurred. "I think you have something there, Il Sunie. The baby's in good condition. Here's three more days' supply of powdered milk. Come back when that is gone."

Thereafter the old man with his beer can and tubing, his limping leg and indomitable cheerfulness, not to mention his husky little grandson, became almost standard equipment at the clinic. He made friends with everyone, particularly with the American soldiers and nurses. Wily old fellow, he knew they paid well for a good laugh!

Eventually Pyong Il was weaned from the beer can. The old man landed a job at the other end of town, and a colorful figure dropped out of view.

JUNE 22. *Early this evening we were just seeing the last of the day's five hundred patients when Father Rush telephoned. "The Sea Serpent with Sister Herman Joseph and Sister Alberta Marie on board is moving toward the dock. Father McGee and I have delegated ourselves a committee of welcome. We'll get the Sisters through the formalities of landing and bring them right up to the Clinic."*

It was 8:30 before they got here. First a little "Thank You" visit to Our Lord in the chapel up the hill. The twenty Carmelite Sisters who still live in two tiny rooms built onto the chapel came out to greet the new arrivals. Then down to our rooms behind the Clinic for a grand old talk. It was late before Sister Mercy reminded us of the five hundred patients who will be at our door tomorrow, and we went to bed. How good it is to be seven Maryknoll Sisters and no longer five!

Sister Herman Joseph, a laboratory technician, began getting her things together to set up shop. We have needed her work badly. Sister is an old Korea hand. She was here in the '30's and was repatriated when World War II broke out. Since 1948 she has been in the Philippines where we have a hospital for sugar plantation workers on Negros Island.

Sister Alberta Marie is a newcomer, a young Sister, twenty-five years old. However, she has a fair grasp on the language; she studied Korean at Yale University for a year. Furthermore, the seven months she has spent waiting in Japan were used for further study of the language. She is to help Sister Rose of Lima in the pharmacy. Sister is all but snowed under, preparing five hundred prescriptions each day.

Sister Alberta Marie tried out her Korean on the youngsters around here and is delighted that they understood her and she, them. They took to her immediately. One can see many happy and fruitful mission years ahead for this young Maryknoll Sister.

6

Death Has a Kind Face

Myong Dok watched his wife die without regret. He could not
help wishing she would be a bit quicker about it.

Late afternoon already. Myong Dok rummaged in the pack
beside him and pulled out a small bamboo container of rice. He
poured some of the dry grains into a bowl, pondered a moment,
and put back a handful. He and the children would have to
make the supply stretch. It was taking so long to reach Pusan.
Then he unstrapped a charcoal stove from a bundle of blankets.

"Pok Ja, get some sticks!" he called out to his oldest child,
a girl of six, "and build a fire." He himself had a bowl in his
hand and went off to find water. Perhaps there was an irrigation
ditch nearby.

"I might as well use this time to get some food into the children," he reasoned to himself. "Then, after she dies, we can get
on the road without delay."

He brought back the water and put the rice to cook in a #10
tin can, salvaged from an American camp somewhere along the
line. Then he poured out a small bowl of water and took it over
to the dying woman. She was unconscious, the death rattle sometimes loud, sometimes soft. He set the bowl gently beside her
and smoothed the sweated hair from her forehead. He moistened
her lips with his finger dipped in the water.

Was it only three weeks since they had left the farm? She

was sick even then. That was why Myong Dok had kept his family on the farm long after his wiser neighbors had evacuated. "We'll get along," he had reassured her. But they hadn't. Bombings and shrapnel. Oxen killed and fields destroyed. At last they knew that they, too, must take to the road.

The first days were not so bad. They had the road practically to themselves, standing aside now and then as military trucks tore past and left them choking with dust. But converging on Pusan—only forty-nine miles from it now!—the road was crowded with refugees all going the same way for the same reason.

Six days ago they had waked to find the baby dead. Well, that was to be expected. The wife had no milk for it and the small life withered and shrank away. Myong Dok hoped that without the baby his wife might have strength to reach their goal—safe Pusan.

Instead, she often fell, rested and struggled to her feet just as before the baby had died. He relieved her of all burdens, strapping the two-year old to his own back, letting Pok Ja carry the slim food stuffs. The sleeping mat and blanket, charcoal stove and bowls he carried himself.

Then came today when she had toppled over, and Myong Dok knew there would be no more risings. He pulled her off the road and with the children's help dragged her behind some rocks. At least, she would have privacy to die in. He would have to leave her body behind; that was plain.

As he waited for the rice to cook, the man noted the families passing and bit his lip in anxiety. It was September and getting chilly at night. In every man and in every woman—almost in every child—he saw a rival for the job he might have if he could get to Pusan before them. Now they were passing him by; each footstep made his chances for some sort of shelter in the oncoming winter just one degree slimmer. They were slim enough already, God knew!

He glanced at the dying woman; she might live for hours yet.

He smothered down the temptation to leave her and go on. Still and all, the chill night out there in the open might not be the best thing for Pok Ja's cough. It might be T.B. "I'll see a doctor about it in Pusan," he promised himself. His common sense jeered back, "Oh yes, you will! And how are you going to pay the doctor?"

The rice was ready now. He dug out the stack of eating bowls from the household pack. Five. Only four needed now. Maybe he could sell that fifth bowl. Hmmmmmm, maybe he could sell two more and let the children eat from the same one. Or, for that matter, why not sell all the bowls? They could all eat from the cooking pot. He saw other refugee families doing it. Less to carry, too. Crockery is heavy. Too heavy for a child to tote all day long on the road. Might be a good idea.

What else could they get along without? Thinking it over, he took up chopsticks and pushed the cooked rice into the bowls. One bowl, two bowls, three bowls. He hesitated before the fourth bowl glancing back at the portions. Awfully skimpy; the children would notice. With a quick decision, he divided the fourth portion into three and put the fourth bowl, empty, back into the household pack.

"Come! Eat!" he shouted to the three children who were half asleep sitting against the rocks. They came running.

Myong Dok went over to his dying wife once more. His glance fell first on her shoes. Not so bad. They might fetch the price of a night's shelter in the next town if they reached there before nightfall. And the comb in her hair—why leave it for somebody else to take? It was worth a good deal of rice.

Ashamed at the thought of stripping his wife even before she breathed her last, he glanced up to her face. And met her half-opened eyes looking at him as clearly as ever. There was a faint catch in the rattling breath. She wanted to say something and could not.

Never mind, he knew what it was. She had often looked at

68

him that way in the past few days, saying, "Don't bother about me. Take the children and go on."

He looked around to see if the children could see them. Husbands and wives in Korea are not demonstrative even before their own children. Then he leaned over her and planted a kiss on her forehead.

"Good wife. Good mother. Thanks!"

She closed her eyes and died.

Sister Agnus Therese writes to her mother:

July 31, 1951

Blackout began just a few minutes ago, so I'm writing this with a flashlight in hand and the kitten purring on my lap.

This can't be much of a letter, Mother. Just enough to let you know I'm all right and that your package of medicines came in good condition. I've filled the Chloromycetin bottle in my good bag—the one you gave me for graduation from Marquette, Mother. The smaller bag you gave me for Christmas several years ago contains my instruments. What good service they have given me!

The crowds are growing by leaps and bounds. On the 19th, we treated 748 patients. On July 26th, the number was up to 900. As I came home from my sick calls on the hills that evening, 150 people were already seated on mats outside on the street. There they spent the night so as to be among the patients we could care for the next morning.

Yesterday, there were 1,003. Now the crowds start collecting for the next day around five o'clock on the afternoon before. We have had to put in a new system. We can take care of only 300 new patients a day. The rest of the 1,000 are old patients coming for medication and check-ups.

At about six A.M. Johnnie Rhee, the gateman, goes out and stamps the clinic seal on the wrists of the first 300 in line. Then when the doors open only those with the seal or who

69

can show readmission cards, are let in. Of course, acutely ill patients for whom a day might mean life or death are admitted at any hour they come.

You may wonder that we stamp the seal on their wrists instead of giving out cards. Well, we have found sharpers out selling cards for admission. We thought this the fairest way; they cannot transfer the seal to somebody else.

August 9, 1951

So many terminal tuberculosis cases! One young lad is in a room with sixteen other young men, all refugees from the North. He was badly beaten by the Communists and is nothing but skin and bones. Many bruises, too. He is riddled with tuberculosis and coughing those deadly germs about all day. Two others in the room are probably active cases, also. All will be if they remain so crowded together.

The case load is so heavy for me now that Sister Kum Ah, one of the Korean Sister nurses, is going out in the mornings to visit tuberculosis cases in the last stages.

Yesterday a woman took me up a mountainside to see a young boy nineteen years old. She felt so sorry for him. His family was all killed; he alone escaped here. He has no home but sleeps out on the ground. He owns only a pair of ragged pants cut off at the knees, and a piece of tar paper which he uses to cover himself with when it rains. The boy has been starved so long that now he cannot eat. There is not an ounce of flesh on him anywhere. He has a very mild and gentle face, but it is heart breaking to see such suffering. I took him some baby food, hoping to start him on something nourishing and thus build him up.

Today being Sunday I had a chance to spend several hours on one patient. It's a terrible skin case, a young man who is pouring pus from every part of his body. He has been in this condition for a month, but without any money, nobody was able to help him.

Knowing the clean-up and dressing would be a major job, we went this morning. Sunday is the only day there is time for so prolonged a task. We worked several hours, but it hardly seems started. His sister is trying to take care of him. She listened so attentively and gratefully to directions for his care that we hope to be able to make some progress. Sister Kum Ah will go over each morning and give him penicillin. Maybe next Sunday we can do another complete dressing job. These poor, poor people!

Torrential rains and the tail of a typhoon does not slow the clinic down any. We are always over 1,000 a day now and often reach into the 1,200's.

August 13

In keeping with the date, we had 1,313 patients today!

August 26

Can't write much. Yesterday 1,500 patients. Love to all.

SEPTEMBER 30. The staff at the Clinic here is growing almost as fast as the patient numbers. Two Maryknoll Sisters, Sisters Dolorosa and Magdalena, arrived from Hong Kong. Both were expelled from China by the Communists a few months ago. Doctor Modrak from the Army Hospital spends his off-duty mornings here putting casts on some of the little children.

Also, Frances Register, who has become a daily assistant at the Clinic, interests many others. Doctor Julio Barbaro, pediatrician in the Army gives almost daily service. Three nurses and two corpsmen came today to offer their services although the small Clinic rooms are hardly big enough to hold all this personnel. Besides our own Americans, a Swedish doctor and nurse help out every day.

Later came the climax. A group from the Jutlandia, a Danish hospital ship, came up to see if they also could help because at

71

present they have not a single patient aboard. A woman doctor, a nurse, a medical student and a Red Cross worker were in the group. They spent the morning observing. The woman doctor is a brain surgeon, but she prefers relief work. She had two years of it in Poland after the last war.

OCTOBER 1. The medical team from the Danish ship was here very early and went quietly to work. They must have wondered at our sense of time, for this is Saturday, "a half workday" we told them. But it began at 8:30 and went straight through to 2:30.

Sister Herman Joseph, who has taken over the clothing-dispensing line, had our men move all the boxes of clothing out from the medical supply room. Just in time! Major Breyfogle of the medical supply depot arrived with a group of men and many boxes of precious medicines that we have been wanting for a long, long time. All of these supplies were obtained by the M.P.'s in raids on the black market.

The innumerable small stalls and shops lining the streets get Army and relief supplies by dubious means and then sell them at high cost. Every now and then—when the black market looks too much like a great storehouse back home—the M.P.'s raid it all. This gives the market dealers a chance to make a fresh start, which they do usually about a half-hour after the raid is over.

Major Breyfogle often stays in the clinic watching the youngsters being treated here. He likes to show us pictures of his wife and two little children. "Everything I am able to do for you," he says, "I do in gratitude to God that my boy and girl are not suffering as these little ones are."

Sister Herman Joseph has her clothes store all organized now. In addition to the injection line, the examination and medicine lines we now start a clothes line, as the children of Pusan take on the hand-me-downs from back home.

What a good sight it is to see the Little Orphan Annies and Tommies who come here being given a good scrub down and presented with two complete sets of clothing. Their brown eyes shine with happiness. For the next week or so Sister Herman Joseph's laboratory will look more like a dry-goods store. The young shoppers really come out looking like new. In between examining slides and doing the rest of the laboratory work, Sister and Frances Register outfit the fashionable young set of Pusan.

If people back home could only see the joy of these youngsters as they don the hand-me-downs! Mothers bring the kiddies to the Clinic now, proud of the suits and dresses that have replaced the rags that were their all.

Some five hundred used baby shirts arrived this afternoon, a gift from Father McGee's parish in New Jersey. They were just what Sister has been looking for to complete the baby layettes. Little Maria, born in a cave just three weeks ago, was the first to come in for a couple of these little shirts.

Myong Dok reveled in a mild wave of prosperity.

The day two months ago when his wife had died on the road was, he hoped, the final all-time low for his family. Since coming to Pusan things had picked up. Source of all his blessings was his job as laborer in an American Army camp.

The salary was not princely, but it sufficed for three meals a day and a matshed which was growing better each week as he added improvements. So when he entered his tiny home this rainy evening, he greeted the children with genuine satisfaction. Pok Ja already had the rice cooking in the battered #10 tin can. "Maybe we can get a real rice pot next week," thought Myong Dok.

"Good girl, Pok Ja!" he praised her. "You're taking after your mother. She'd be proud of you."

As he patted her cheek, she felt hot to his touch. "That afternoon fever again!" he noted to himself. "I'll have to get her to a doctor. Well, sometime I'll take a day off and we'll go to the *Su Nyo Nim's* clinic down there."

Yes, indeed, things were beginning to grow normal. Pil Songie, the four-year-old boy, was setting out the bowls for evening rice. Little Kae Ok was too young to help; she was over in a corner asleep on the pile of rags which formed the family bed for the present.

Myong Dok bestirred himself to collect every container he had and they were many. He was among the most diligent scroungers in the Army dump piles. As a farmer, he had always had a fondness for rain; as a refugee, he knew it for a real blessing from Heaven. He ran out into the cold wet night and set out his treasures—two five-gallon gasoline tins and any number of large cans. The more water he collected tonight, the less he had to buy from the water peddlers.

Once outside, standing there in the rain, he looked up at the overhanging ledge of the clay mountainside. It jutted out far; his home and three others were under it. Two months ago when he had started building his matshed there, it had seemed a friendly sort of thing. "When winter comes," he told his neighbor, Pak Sai In, "that ledge will shelter our homes from cold winds. We won't be having an ondol in the house, you know— at least not this year! We'll be glad to be in under something."

He hurried into the shack shaking off the rain. The gusts of wind seemed stronger; autumn was surely setting in. He congratulated himself once more on taking up his residence under the protection of that ledge. His home was not built to withstand typhoons.

Half an hour later, when evening rice was over, he stripped himself down to his shorts. No use getting his clothes wet. As long as the storm lasted he intended to go out every now and then to bring in his catch of rain. The big crock in the corner would be filled by morning with fresh water. Thank the Lord of Heaven for rain! The Lord of Heaven responded to his gratitude and sent more and more rain. Several times, Myong Dok rose from his sleep and brought in the good fresh rain-water. It was very early in the morning, in the grey before dawn, that he first noticed. . . .

74

It was a wild stream of water tearing down from the mountaintop and running over the ledge. It poured like Niagara off the far side away from his shack; boulders and shrub-roots in the rush indicated its force. A stream like that could loosen the whole ledge and bring about a landslide.

Myong Dok ran over to Sai In's house and banged wildly at the door.

"Sai In! Sai In! The ledge! Get up!"

Sai In pulled open the door. He, too, saw the danger. "Chol Chun has a shovel," he suggested. "Let's get it and divert the flow away from us."

The two men ran to Chol Chun's shack. Soon every neighbor in the area was out with tools—anything at all which would dig the earth. The almost naked men scrambled up the mountainside above the ledge. Two or three pushed boulders into place to form a sort of dam until the trench could be dug.

Like a wild man, Myong Dok pulled up roots and prepared the way for Chol Chun wielding his shovel. He thought of getting the children out of the house. "No. At least they're dry where they are," he decided. Besides the ledge still looked strong, and, of course, it had stood up under many another hard rain. Moreover, he noted two hopeful signs—the sun was coming up and the rain was lessening.

Then, suddenly it happened. Chol Chun was standing on the ledge when he felt the ground go out from under him. The torrent, pushing aside the flimsy little dam, carried him on a wild ride for a thousand feet or more. Myong Dok was not far behind him. Luckily, neither was hurt. They scrambled to their feet. Slipping and sliding over the still moving wet clay, they ran back.

"Pok Ja! Pok Ja!" cried Myong Dok. "Pil Songie! Kae Ok!" He could see just a corner of the shack protruding from the landslide.

Chol Chun was not so fortunate. His wife and his house were buried completely. The other men ran down, carefully skirting the ragged hole in the mountainside where the protecting ledge had once been. Their own houses were intact. Women and children came running out into the cold dawn. Their men were safe. One woman had rice ready for them all. But the men had borrowed the shovel and were digging frantically through the wet clay where Chol Chun's house had been. "Careful! You may cut her with that thing!" Chol Chun warned them. "Go easy." He himself was digging with his hands, like a dog.

It was he who found her. First her leg and on up to her shoulder. The roofbeam of the shack—not a heavy piece of lumber, but a deadly weapon when hurled by tons of sliding clay—lay square across her head. No doubt about it, she was dead. Chol Chun watched his neighbors put the earth back over her. He himself was too heartsick to help.

Myong Dok was running toward his own frail home. As he struggled through the slippery mud, calling the children's names, his heart leaped to see Pok Ja backing out from the ruins, pulling Pil Songie out by his arms. The boy did not move.

"Where's Kae Ok?" he shouted.

Dazed, Pok Ja faced his oncoming figure and pointed inside the half-buried hut. The father came slipping toward her and went inside. Little Kae Ok was unconsicous; her legs were caught in the debris, her ribs and chest caved in on one side, and an ugly gash along her cheek and over the top of her head. The big water-jar had toppled over when the wall was shoved in. In crashing to the floor, a piece of the heavy crockery banged against her small ribs. Another piece cut sharply into her head. Myong Dok extricated her as gently as he could, and carried her out into the dawning day. She was still breathing, but it was labored.

Sai In approached him. He picked up Pil Songie, who was still unconscious but not visibly hurt.

"Come on," he said. "I'll help you get them to the Clinic."

OCTOBER 4. *The night's drizzling rain turned into a wind-blown* downpour in the early morning hours. Nonetheless, two hundred patients slept outside in the lines last night. As many as possible had crowded into the waiting room the G.I.'s have built for them.

As the wind mounted high and water poured down the mountainsides, we feared for the refugees living in tiny matsheds.

Soon after dawn two half-naked men dripping with mud prevailed upon the night watchman to let them in. They carried in their arms two small children taken from a shack crushed by a landslide. The little girl still had a heartbeat but lived only a few minutes after Sister Mercy had given her fading life an eternal remedy.

The other child, a boy of four, unconscious when brought in, responded well to stimulants. He was suffering mainly from shock. A third child, a six-year-old girl, was remarkably self-possessed. It was she who had pulled her younger brother out of their crumbling home. The father suspects she may have T.B. and will bring her back tomorrow for examination. He asked for "kitchen yak"—cough medicine—for her. We outfitted them all with American hand-me-down clothes. Carrying the dead child, the little party trudged back up the mountain—no, not to their home, for that isn't any more, but to some other matshed where kindly neighbors will shelter them until a new home can be built. The father is heart-broken. His wife and small baby died on the road a few months ago.

7

Agneta, Little Lamb

All that day Sister Peter had kept saying to herself, "Tonight I must do it." The task was long overdue. She had put it off, hoping each morning that good news might come, and knowing each night that it probably never would.

An experience today—not much different from many other experiences, though—had formed her resolution.

In the afternoon, around three o'clock, a man had crawled into the Clinic on his hands and knees. His ancient snowy haired mother had walked tiredly beside him. He had been carried to Tae Chong Dong Road in a jiggy frame—that is, a sort of wooden harness on the back of a Korean porter—all the way from Yong Do, at least a three-hour journey. The jiggy-frame man, having been paid off, had deposited him at the street level. The man had crawled up the steps and over to the door on his hands and knees. Advanced T.B., certainly terminal.

Why had he come? Poor fellow, he had left his shelter under a bridge—his home for the past ten months—confident that if he could but manage to reach the Maryknoll Sisters' Clinic, he might stay there and await death in peace. Like so many others, he thought the Clinic was a hospital where he could have a bed and in-patient care.

Sister Mercy had given him medicine. She got blankets, a supply of food and had slipped some money into his mother's hand

—more than enough to pay for a jiggy-frame ride back to their underbridge shelter. It was the best she could do, and she turned her attention to the long line awaiting her.

Late that evening, after the patients had cleared off, Johnnie Rhee, the gateman, had come to the convent door.

"That man and his mother never went," he had reported. "They're out there on the street. Going to stay all night, I guess."

"Ask Sister Peter if she can spare two Korean dinners for them," Sister Mercy had told Johnny as she went out to see what condition her patient was in.

Sister Peter and her Korean Sisters of the Mother of Perpetual Help had been at supper. Dressed in conventual black and white, looking like nuns as they are always pictured—with a bit of starchy white around the face, full skirts, long sleeves—they sat at the long low table in true Korean fashion while eating, kneeling first and gracefully sitting back on their heels. They wielded chopsticks and bowls silently, listening to Sister Man Dok (Sister Hope in English) read from a hand-written Korean manuscript. It was the manuscript which prodded Sister Peter's conscience that evening.

"Sister Agneta's last work for us!" she said to herself. "Yes, I must finish writing tonight."

When Johnnie Rhee had come with his message, Sister Peter slipped out of the refectory, through the kitchen and down in the chilly evening to the street bearing two big bowls of rice and sauce. Sister Mercy was beside the sick man.

"He's really comfortable here," she had told Sister Peter. "He's warm, wrapped in the blankets, and free from pain, thanks to the medicine. Let's give them a good meal and let them stay overnight in the waiting room. Tomorrow, perhaps, you can get him into the Korean Hospital for Civilians. You know people there, Sister Peter, since you visit it nearly every day. Maybe you can pull a few strings for him."

So it was that Sister Peter, the old woman and the dying man

79

were left together. So it was that The Past burst upon Sister Peter and set her mind and heart in a whirl.

For they were old acquaintances. Thirty years before, when Sister Peter, fresh from Normal School, was starting out as a teacher in northern Korea, not far from the Manchurian border, this man was a child in her class.

"Bright as a button," she remembered silently. "And what plans his mother had for him then! See what they have come to."

"You are Mun Poh Pai, then!" exclaimed the old mother. "What happened to you? After a few years, we saw you no more. And yet all of us used to say, 'Ah, that Mun Poh Pai! She'll be a principal in our schools someday.'"

"I became as you see me now, Sin Tok. I became a Sister."

"Ai Go!" the old lady exclaimed. She was full of rice now, warm and comfortable. Meeting an old friend put the top on a very satisfactory situation. "But you are not like the other Sisters. They dress in grey, wear pointed caps, eat foreign food. I used to hear in Pyongyang in the old days, that they wear street shoes inside their house. They're good people, no doubt, but their ways are very odd."

"Yes," Sister Peter agreed. "Most of them are Americans, which accounts for a lot. They belong to the Maryknoll family which goes all over the world. We are Korean Sisters and we intend to do work only in our own beloved Korea. And yet we owe our beginnings to them.

"The Catholic Church is a mother, Sin Tok. She is constantly bringing into the world new organizations and societies. Usually she puts each new infant congregation under the care of an older one so that the young Sisters learn the ways of religious life from someone more experienced."

The old lady shook her head sagely. "Very wise! That's the way it ought to be, Mun Poh Pai. It's just what I would do myself. The old should teach the young."

"So when our Korean congregation began, Sin Tok, some

Maryknoll Sisters were put in charge of us to teach us the ways of right living as daughters of the Church. That was in 1932 in Pyongyang."

"And to think I didn't know a thing about it! And me right in the city!" Sin Tok was mystified. "But you had not joined the group then, had you? It seems to me I saw you at the graduation of my younger son and that was in 1934."

"Ah yes," Sister Peter remembered. "So it was! But I had it in mind then. The next year I came to present myself as a victim to do God's Will forever and ever."

"Ai Go!" the old lady was horrified. "Not that! That would be a wretched life, entirely. Much better, I think, if the gods do what I want. That's what I pray for. And you, with such a wonderful future ahead of you!"

Sister Peter smiled. What was the use of trying to explain the truth of "My yoke is sweet and My burden light?" It would be incomprehensible to Sin Tok as it was to millions of others. The old lady went on, "What sort of people were they that put such nonsense into your head?"

"Beginning with us was Sister Genevieve, an American Maryknoll Sister. And with her was a young Korean Maryknoll Sister, Sister Agneta. It was she who became our beloved mother."

Sin Tok dismissed them both from her mind. "I didn't know either of them," she said emphatically. "Tell me now, Mun Poh Pai, about your brother, the alderman, Mun Ki Poong. What happened to him when the Russians took over northern Korea in 1945? Ai Go! Ai Go! That was when hard times came to our poor country! And we thought ourselves badly off under the Japanese!"

The two old friends talked on many subjects while the sick man slept or turned restlessly. Yet, when Sister Peter took the two empty bowls and trudged back to the Korean convent on the hill top, it was Sister Agneta's face which filled her mind. And her ears were filled with Sister Agneta's groans as she lay on her injured spine jolting in the ox-cart.

81

"Tonight, I will finish the letter," she promised.

The other Sisters had gone to bed after singing their evening prayers and then unrolling their sleeping mats of rice straw to spread on the floor. House furnishings in a Korean home are simple and yet adequate. No clumsy chairs, tables or beds. Rather, a workroom by day—or a diningroom or any sort of room—can be converted into a dormitory by the simple process of unrolling the sleeping mats.

Sister Peter saw them all safely fixed for the night. She paused by one who seemed tired out by the heavy work in the Marine laundry where several of them were employed. "Take an hour's extra rest," she told her. So it was that Sister Agneta had taught her. A superior must care for the health of all the Sisters.

Then, alone in her tiny office, she took out a sheaf of fine Korean papers, thin as onion skin, lined and delicately water-marked with an all-over flower design. Already she had written much of Sister Agneta's story. She dreaded to finish it, hoping that before it was mailed to Maryknoll some good news might turn up. She read what she had written so far:

Most honorable Mother General!

The fate of your beloved daughter Sister Agneta is a nightmarish mystery to us. Only God knows what happened to her and whether she be alive or dead. It is already four long months since we lost our dear Mother.

Ever since we lost her on October 4, 1950, I have tried my utmost to find what became of her. Two weeks later, Pyongyang was liberated by the United Nations. Then I set out in more active earnestness to search all the probable places she might be.

There being such a tragically great number of places where patriots were slaughtered, I walked five to eight miles each day to every place of killing and every place of burial, thinking that our Mother, too, might have met such a fate. I wished to find at least the body so that I might be able to bury it as best I could.

At the same time we Sisters were extremely busy repairing our convent which was destroyed when Pyongyang was liberated by the Americans. All the time we were settling ourselves again, we were in search of our Mother.

On December 1, 1950, Pyongyang was again threatened by Communists, for the Red Chinese were pouring into Korea to aid the Russians. During the night, we cleared out the household and retreated from the city on the dawn of December 2nd.

We had no earthly belongings, for we had been fleeing from place to place all summer. We arrived in Pusan with but the clothes on our backs and our Office Books.

Through the eternal mercy of God, we are now staying in the house of the Maryknoll Sisters, meeting expenses by taking in sewing and laundry for the soldiers. Living in this way, I have not found much free time.

During these months I have tried innumerable times to write to you, but I cannot say how often I took up my pen to begin a letter, only to find all turned black before me and I could not hold back the tears that blinded me.

I tried my best with mental agony throughout the years of their tyranny (the Communist occupation of Northern Korea) to protect our Mother. I hoped to be able to prevent the fate that had to be.

Our Mother, your Sister Agneta, was a saintly person who always kept Christ living within us. What efforts she exerted to teach our ignorance! She also took care of the innumerable financial hardships of our convent. All these hardships she embraced with a smile. I, who have been with her for fourteen years, was luckier than any other person, but this only makes the wound of her passing the deeper within me.

Oh most honorable Mother General! We honor Sister Agneta for her deep love for her own congregation, Maryknoll.

Our most respected Mother used to keep on her desk a picture of the altar at Maryknoll and also a photograph of you. But after May, 1949, when Bishop Hong was taken to prison, she put away your photograph because it was the picture of an American and we did not know on what day nor at what time we might be raided.

I cannot attempt to relate on paper all of our Mother's life since World War II began, but let me tell you roughly of our life in those years of warfare and since.

On December 13, 1941, five days after World War II broke out, Sister Agneta was appointed Superior of our Convent of the Mother of Perpetual Help. Being a Korean, she was not evacuated from the country and sent back to the United States when the American Maryknoll Sisters were sent away from us. In His mercy, God left her to us that we might not be entirely without guidance in His ways. There were thirty-seven of us Sisters of Our Mother of Perpetual Help then and we stayed at this figure throughout the war.

In 1945 we were all elated that peace had come. How were we to guess that such sorrow would follow? Because of the aggression of the Russian soldiers who soon swept over the city of Pyongyang we had to shed our Sister's habits and scatter. However, after several weeks we ventured back and resumed our convent life. But not with the freedom of before. We could not open the windows even during the summer but had to keep them always bolted. We could not have any lights in the night and trembled in perpetual fear. We lived in this way for several years.

After Russia, in appearance, had taken its hands off the government, the North Korean Communists began their oppression in real earnest. From the beginning of 1947, we had no communication with the world outside of North Korea. We could get no messages from Maryknoll, not even from Seoul which used to be but five hours away by railroad.

Their gradually tightening trickery increased during 1948 but our Mother was able to bring us all—we were forty-four by then—through each new ruse. Early in 1949, all evils increased, as they actively stretched a hand against Catholics. We felt that the terrifying and oppressive atmosphere about us would never clear.

Their daily visits for questioning, their personal investigation of our Mother, were hard to bear. They held it much against her that she had lived in America for three years. Also they made it a crime that she was well educated, being a graduate of Sacred Heart College in Tokyo.

Because there was nothing they could find wrong about the convent, they utilized a person of insufficient faith. The person's name was Peter. I had reprimanded him once for some great wrong deed he kept repeating. As a revenge for this he had the priest, the catechist and me arrested and jailed. The priest and I were confined for about thirty hours and the catechist—our good Joseph Pak—for ten days. He was put through all kinds of torture. They also offered him a bribe to spy on church doings, but he, being a faithful Catholic, refused to do such a thing. He was at last released.

On May 8, 1949, Bishop Dok Won Shin (Bishop of Wonsan in Northern Korea, staffed by German Benedictine priests) was arrested. The Korean priests and brothers as well as the Germans were taken with him. The nuns in the Wonsan convent, also. Ah, you must know how we felt at the time.

We knew that it would now be our turn. Working through the nights, we disposed of everything. We put away books belonging to the Maryknoll Fathers, the Sisters' suitcases they had left behind, any books in English or other such things that appeared American. We searched from the basement to the attic, disposing of articles and burning everything that had to be destroyed. Like thieves in the night, when all was quiet in sleep our Mother and a few other Sisters took the important papers, books and other things to a safe place,

85

six or seven miles away. Thus we worked nearly every night for many months.

On May 14, 1949, Bishop Hong (Bishop of Pyongyang. The convent was a short distance outside the city.) came on foot, with his eighteen-year-old houseboy and a shepherd dog, on official business. He had a talk with our Mother and departed at about five o'clock; a boy had come with a letter telling him to go to the city at once.

The next day we learned that the Bishop had disappeared. There was also no trace of either the boy or the dog. Some said that the head of the Political Defense Department had arrested the Bishop on his way back to the city.

On June 10th, Father Louis Kim of Kwanhuri was arrested. At the same time, Father Matthias Chuch and his catechist, Mr. Kang, were likewise taken.

On June 27th, several of us were to have made our perpetual vows, the final step in consecrating our lives to Almighty God. But in view of conditions it was thought wiser to delay the step. Therefore, in the midst of tears, we once more renewed our vows for another year.

Father Mark Suk of Kanggoh was beaten in the night of July 8th and taken captive. Then they took Father Timothy Pak of Sungiori, Father Boniface Suh, Father Alex Lee of Kirimwi, Father Andrei Chang who stayed at the bishop's house, and a seminarian. They were all arrested in the night and taken to we know not where. Their churches were used as the town hall or theater or some other gathering place.

Now our convent became the special object of the Communist's spying. They arrested people coming for confession and Mass, summoned the Sister-portress and questioned her as to what people visited our convent. They made us write our autobiographies, hand in our personal histories, and so on. They did not allow parishioners to come near the convent. If anyone should come, we were questioned as to what we had talked about.

86

Under these circumstances, our financial condition was, of course, bad, but, more, we had absolutely no peace of mind. Even in the midst of all this, however, our Mother Agneta translated books we needed in our spiritual life and laid down one by one good rules for our convent life, not neglecting anything. She was weak to begin with. Added to this was incessant work and the circumstances of the times. She fell ill and could neither sleep nor eat much from the end of January, 1950. She complained especially of her legs, saying that they were numb and felt as though ants were crawling up and down them. I was instructed by a doctor to keep her in her room and nurse her.

It was at this time she heard that the Mother General of the Maryknoll Convent wished her to come through the terrible iron curtain which encircled our poor country of Korea. After hearing this, she tried hard to get well and made plans to go south. A guide was to come and help her to slip across the border. Sometimes I hoped that our convent would be dissolved by order of the government in order to give our Mother the chance to leave.

About this time police started to make night-lodging investigations, coming at night usually between midnight and two A.M. They went from room to room in search of anyone who might be sleeping here without first registering with the police. This was actually only an excuse to see the place, for they suspected that we had some secret chamber or radio equipment hidden somewhere.

Luckily, or perhaps unluckily, on May 4, 1950, we were summoned to a place called Sunan. There they told us they wished to talk about our buildings. It was useless. We offered them our buildings without any protest. They were to take over on the 15th of May.

At first we thought to continue our religious life in another convent, but we learned that it was really because they disapproved of our group life that they took our buildings. So we finally set about dissolving our convent in the midst of tears.

The guide who was to take Sister Agneta across the border to South Korea appeared on the 9th or 10th of May. "I have to go to Seoul hurriedly," he told us. "I will return for you about twenty days after the dissolution of the convent. It will be more convenient for me and will also appear more natural since by that time all the Sisters will be scattered." So our Mother put off the thought of escaping until early June.

On the last night before we were all to leave, our Mother called us to her and talked to us for the last time, giving us motherly advice, saying that due to unavoidable reasons the convent had to be dispersed. After it was dispersed, no one was to look for her but to go to me—unworthy Sister Peter— for any advice or help.

On May 14th our Sisters were dressed in civilian clothes. On that day we turned our backs upon the house of God and each went her own way. The Political Defense Officer of our county alerted the Political Defense Officer of each Sister's home town to expect her arrival.

Here I would like to tell you that Joseph Pak had become a member of the Communist intelligence in order to help us. Pretending to spy on this church and convent and gaining their trust, he learned their schemes and ambitions of which he secretly informed us. Because of this, we were able to avoid any misfortune and to dissolve our convent without mishap. Our Mother, Sister Agneta, too, came to trust in him, discussing difficult problems with him. He staked his life and helped us daringly. Until the end, he was a great comfort to us.

Our Mother, while waiting for the guide to return and take her south, went to a relative's house with only her single suit of clothing. She was afraid, however, to leave for the south

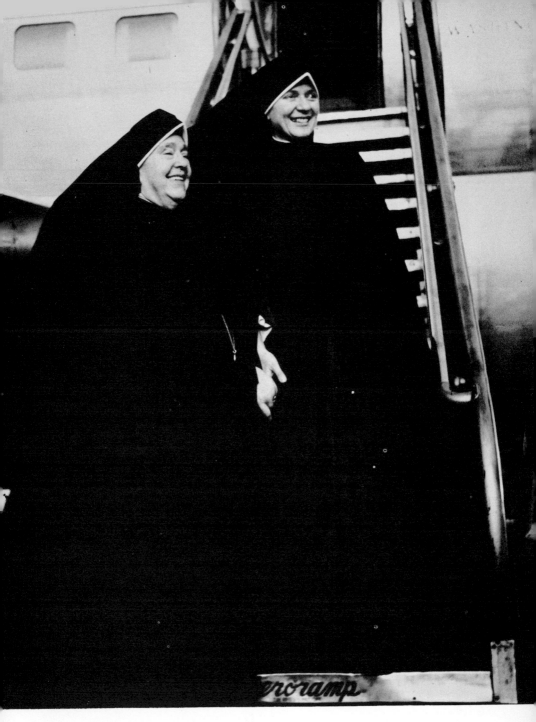

Off to Korea where "the incident" was raging. Mother Mary Joseph gave a parting squeeze of the hand as Sister Mercy stepped aboard her plane in December, 1950. As Foundress of the Maryknoll Sisters, Mother had trained and sent out hundreds of missionaries in the 30 years previous.

Both are wearing black mantles, covering the usual Maryknoll grey habit.

USIS KOREA

High on the hill side property is the mausoleum built by the former owner so that he might rest in his beloved garden. Sister Alberta Marie lies now right behind the little white fence.

This family slept in the unused sewer pipes, crawling into them at night for whatever warmth they could provide.

Dressed thus, this mother brought her baby on a December day. The sun was bright, but the winds blew cold.

Literally millions of refugees trudged up these narrow steps to the Clinic from the street. Later, Army engineers constructed a driveway to replace them. An enterprising refugee built his shack on the ledge; vendors set up shop to feed the waiting multitudes.

Smallpox! When cases came in, doctor and nurse went out to vaccinate children in the patient's home district. It was fairly prevalent in Pusan.

Pyong Il rests against the gatepost awaiting his turn. Forty winks will help to pass the time.

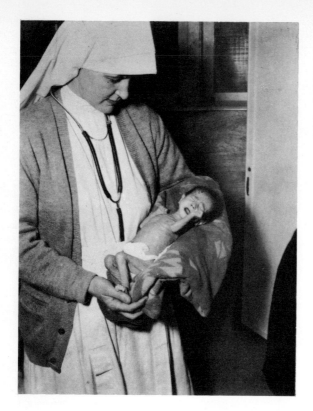

Looking at starved babies like this, Sister Agnus Therese thought gratefully of her bouncing niece at home. She called this one, "Never-Say-Die Joey."

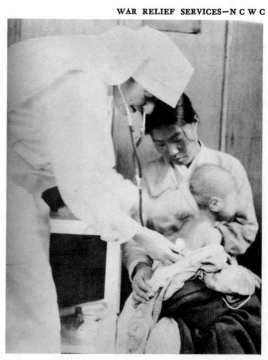

As a doctor, Sister Mercy is quick but thorough in examination. Korean mothers had implicit trust in her diagnoses.

Tuberculosis of the spine takes a heavy toll in malnourished bodies. Here Sister Agnus Therese prepares to put this lad in a cast. He will have to be in one for years.

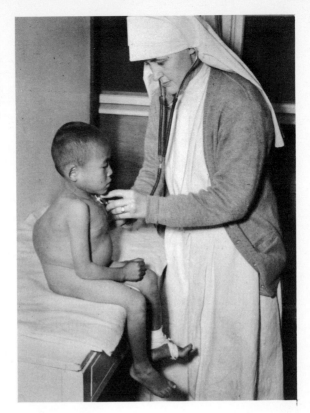

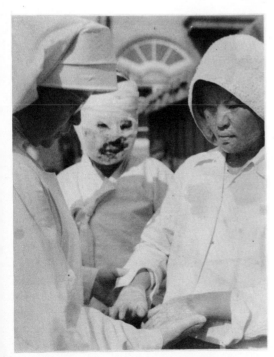

Sister Rose of Lima checks on this patient's burned hands. "The Phantom of the Opera," gets into the picture, too, proud of his new bandage job.

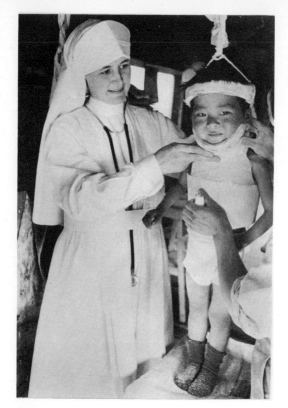

More than 350 children in casts came regularly for clean-up and check-up. This little fellow seems to like the process.

"The Black Beetle" brought aid much farther and faster than was possible in the early months.

In the homes of burlap and cardboard, lay human beings too sick to come for aid. The afternoons were spent visiting them.

Blood poisoning and a man-gled hand. Sister Mercy tries not to hurt too much as she examines the case.

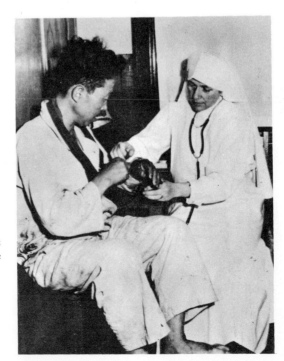

Each of these women had waited all night. It was hard to choose the most urgent cases for immediate treatment.

Many Army and Navy doctors as well as United Nations personnel spent their free time in the Clinic. Here are a Swedish doctor and nurse.

USIS KOREA

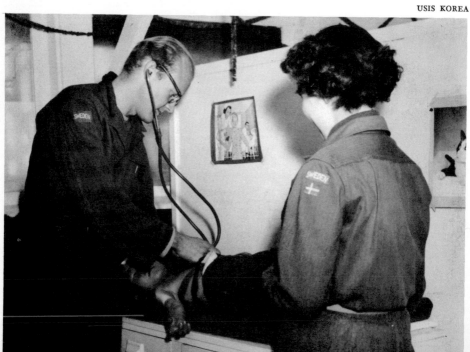

Christmas party for the orthopedic cases brought wan smiles to some faces; others were too dazed to know what Christmas should mean.

This Korean Sister of Perpetual Help escaped from Communist North Korea. Here at Pusan she devotes her life to aid other refugees.

Marquette grants a Doctor of Science, Honoris Causa, to Sister Mercy amidst an ovation which rocked the auditorium, in June, 1952. She took the opportunity to enlist support for the Korean work.

Cardinal Spellman's Christmas visits brought cheer to the soldiers and financial aid to the Clinic. Here, Sister Rose of Lima and Sister Mercy listen to what seems to be a tall tale.

"Our Gang" lines up for the camera—and it takes eight Sisters to keep them still for 1/50th of a second.

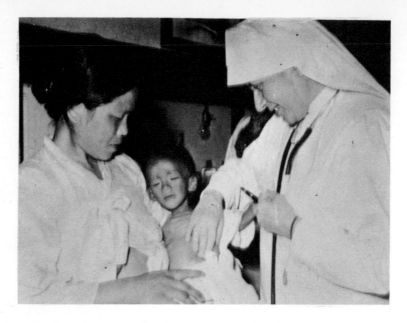

One has to be so gentle with these emaciated little bodies. Sister Mercy watches the reactions as she examines.

Sister Dolorosa keeps the records straight as thousands of patients mill past her desk.

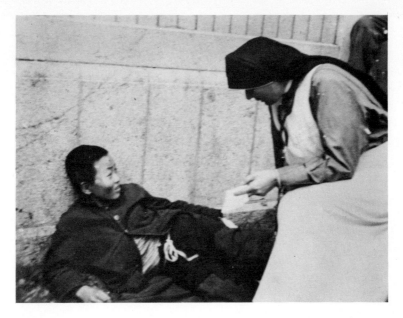

He had dragged himself to the Clinic wall but had not the strength to go in. Sister Mercy takes the case right there on the pavement.

Sister Herman Joseph makes giving so joyous that the getting is all the merrier. Here the "clothes line" reaches out the window.

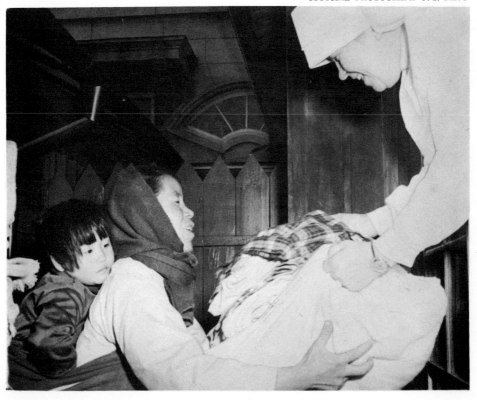

Farewell! There were speeches and photographs. General Whitcomb looks quizzical as Sister Mercy listens to the Mayor of Pusan.

A Peanut Butter Baby comes in for check-up. Sister can remember when this little tyke was a scrawny infant. Mama is proud, not only of him, but also of Little Brother who hangs out behind.

Breaking in a laboratory assistant. Sister Herman Joseph realizes the long years ahead before the Korean people will recover from the shock and disintegration of the war years.

On to the future! Sister Angelica pours the first shovelful of concrete into the new hospital's foundation. Thus began her tremendous task of building and equipping a 165-bed hospital.

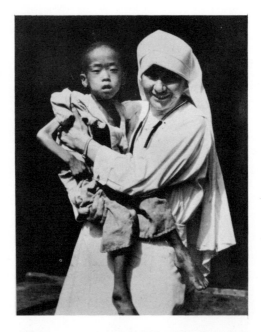

This boy was once crippled through tuberculosis of the bone. Now he faces the future valiantly.

directly from her relative's house and thus subject that good person to suspicion and questioning.

"I have always said in questioning that I am sick," she said, "so it might be best to go to a hospital first and leave from there."

With her escape in mind, she managed to be hospitalized in Pyongyang's biggest hospital, the National Central Hospital, on May 23rd. She was in a ward with fifteen other patients. She always bore their ignorant and filthy noisiness with a happy smile, looking after their comfort and helping them always as an angel of love.

They did not know what to say of our Mother. Some said she was not of this world, that she was a heavenly being. Adults and children alike loved to talk to her and to receive her help and nursing. People who were to have a big operation would feel safe if she consented to nurse them after it.

She had no rest in this way. On the contrary, with all their demands on her, her health suffered. But passing the days in doing good things, she only waited for the guide to come for her. But he finally did not appear at all.

She had to leave the hospital on June 19, 1950, and went out to Nampo where Father Paul Cho had invited her to stay. She was here when war broke out June 25th. That very morning, Father Paul Cho was arrested. The remaining five priests who had not been arrested as yet were all taken that day.

Sister Agneta returned to the city of Pyongyang on the 29th. She had been given instructions by Father Paul Cho before he was taken prisoner. "If war breaks out," he told her, "I will be arrested. I want you to go to Pyongyang. Troops from South Korea will come within a few days to liberate the city. When this happens, there are a few Catholic young men primed to break open the prison gates and free the Bishop and priests inside. They will need help from you. Be sure to be at the prison gates to welcome our Bishop when he

89

is freed. He has been in prison for more than a year now and will need you."

The fact that Bishop Hong and his priests were in the Pyongyang prison was an extreme secret. Someone—I will not reveal his name—had learned of the until-then-completely-unknown whereabouts of Bishop Hong. Our Mother had been informed before and I, too, was aware of it. The other Sisters knew nothing of it.

The weeks passed. The bombing became more intense. Everyone was evacuating. The city at this time was in a dizzy state. In North Korea all men between eighteen and fifty-six were drafted. Young boys and girls were all pulled into the Army. The remaining population were always called out by civilian labor enforcement units. The young people, wishing to avoid the Army, hid in the mountains in dug-out caves or inside ceilings. There was hardly any house that did not hide a son, daughter or husband. Such a hectic state! People hiding, people searching for the ones in hiding, people running away, etc. How could we, who were objects of particular suspicion, ask anyone to take us in? Even our relatives avoided us; Catholics who used to welcome us were now all afraid even to meet us.

We began running from place to place, not wishing to stay long anywhere lest we bring trouble to our hosts. Our Mother's legs became much worse. On the first day, she could walk for a half-hour but after that she had to be carried in a bicycle trailer. Later, her legs became useless; she had to go from place to place in an ox-cart. Over the steep and ragged mountain paths, the ox-carts could just barely travel.

Our longest stay was in a Catholic village several days' journey from Pyongyang. Although she suffered from dysentery for about two weeks, our Mother recovered some of her health. She would play with the children and tell them stories. She also said the Divine Office as she used to do at the Maryknoll convent.

90

No one visited us nor did we have a radio. We knew nothing of the world situation. At first Joseph Pak came now and then, but he feared people might suspect that we were making some secret communication. He stopped his visits. From then on no one at all came.

However, on September 4th, Joseph Pak came once more bearing terrifying news. He said that the government knew where Sister Agneta was. They intended to make her broadcast through the radio, since she was well known to Catholics in Korea. She was to tell our Catholics that North Korean politics were right and true. "I explained and argued warmly to them," Joseph Pak said, "saying that nuns can take no part in political affairs. They will not listen. They will even make you do it by force if necessary." Respectful Mother General! You can picture how great was our fear and worry because of this news.

Our Mother passed that night in agonizing worry. We could not stay in that peaceful village any longer but must leave early the next morning. But where were we to go?

If we simply disappeared, our host would face a great deal of trouble. As long as our cruel masters were out for us they were sure to get us eventually. We could not escape their terrifying political observation. But bombing was very heavy in Pyongyang and the city was almost empty of people; our Mother decided to go back.

The ox-cart came for us at the appointed time, even before the day grew light. That morning, however, she hurt her back while rising. The good Catholics and our kind host persuaded her to remain with them. Thus it was that she finally did not go.

After that for more than three weeks it was very quiet but our Mother's back pained her very much. She could not rise from her bed and spent her days and nights in agony.

On September 28th Joseph Pak came again, but with good news. Seoul had been liberated! The Communist Army *was being destroyed. "I will come back for you when liberation comes," he said.*

Sister Peter put down the sheaf of papers and sighed. This was the hardest part. To end on a cheerful note like this and then to be obliged to tell the rest of the story. But she took up her pen and began to write.

Oh most respectful Mother General! Then came the morning of October 4th.

A messenger came from the neighborhood civilian labor office commanding us all to come at once to cut trees for the military. Sending Sister Helena, a young Sister who stayed with us, we asked her to explain that we could not come.

But at eleven o'clock the neighborhood Party Cell Chief appeared and angrily asked why we had not come when told. I said, "As you see, that person is in bed with a hurt back and I not only cannot leave such a sick person, but I cannot walk well because of rheumatism. Will you please go and make excuses for us?"

Upon hearing this, he told us both to go together by ox-cart to the nearest town, Sunan, and get doctor's certificates. Somehow, I felt there was more to this than appeared on the surface. Sister Agneta laughed at my fears. "Nothing is going to happen," she said.

After lunch I intended to go alone for the certificates and set out walking. But I could not get the thought out of my mind that they were up to some evil scheme. So I turned around and went back. Then I hid the Divine Office book, also Sister Agneta's books in English and any other article they disliked. I said the rosary with our Mother.

In the late afternoon Sister Helena had not returned from the conscription gang cutting down trees. I was preparing to make supper for the three of us when someone banged loudly on the door and burst into the house shouting, "Is this the house of Lee Shung On (Sister Agneta)?"

Oh, I was extremely afraid but assuming a calm appearance, I went out slowly to find an officer and a man in plain clothes. An ox-cart was waiting outside.

"Whom are you looking for?"

"We want Lee Chung On."

"Where do you come from?"

"From the military mobilization office. Lee Chung On has knowledge of medicine and nursing. She is a person needed by the country."

I begged and pleaded with them saying that this ailment of our Mother needed no special treatment but just rest. Besides, she could not be moved now. But with no human feelings, or justice or morals, they insisted. At first they told me to come along, too, but later they said it was Lee Chung On they wanted and they had no use for me.

After arguing like this for about two hours, our Mother was taken from me without compassion by their evil hands. They called out the neighbors and made them carry our Mother's bed onto the ox-cart. The neighbors said never a word. When I saw how quietly they carried our Mother whom they loved so well, I felt resentment and pity. I realized again the misery of the weak.

Oh please forgive me, General Superior! This is how our Sister Agneta departed. She was not clothed properly but was loaded on the ox-cart covered with a quilt. As she was pulled along the narrow hill trail, suffering much from the jolting, she cried "Lord have mercy upon us!" and in a loud voice repeated ejaculations.

The time was about eight in the evening. The world was wrapped in dusk and the only sound was that of the ox-cart jogging down the quiet mountain trail. Together with it could be heard, only close by, the groaning and sound of her prayers. Oh miserable sight! My heart seemed to shatter and break

93

into a thousand pieces. It seemed pitiless to me that the ground did not cleave open.

I walked behind her but she bade me not to follow and I turned back. I sent a man out immediately to follow that ox-cart. But after going about two and a half miles he returned saying that it was near the curfew hour and the sentries were very severe.

Sister Helena, who had gone out to work that morning, still did not return. The twilight had faded and my heart grew heavier as the dark night enfolded all around me.

Oh, my honorable General Superior! How can I find words to describe it? I felt as if I were tossed by the waves and going insane. Yet it was only by quiet meditation that I could bear my insufferable sadness. Sister Helena came in; together we wept!

Because they said they were taking our Mother to Sunan, the next dawn Sister Helena and I started out. On the way we met Joseph Pak. When he heard our news, he looked thunderstruck and said he had had not the faintest idea of this scheme of theirs.

"Go to the intelligence officer you know and get help for her," I told him. He came back very soon.

"Sister Agneta, according to the national plan, is directly under the National Police. We in the local office can do nothing," he reported. "But you, Sister Peter, should hurry away. There is an order out to arrest you today. Do not stay around making useless efforts over Sister Agneta."

An order for my arrest? This did not affect me at all. I might be taken where our Mother was! Having no place else to go, I hurried on to Suhpo to my old home. Here, before my blood mother, I cried my heart out.

The next day I went to Pyongyang. Everyone had evacuated because of the heavy bombing. I found out that Bishop Hong and all the priests under him had been taken elsewhere on October 3rd. I wondered if our Mother on the next day was taken to be with them. What a comfort it would be to her. The more I think of it, the more I can imagine how our Mother's heart must have ached to be captured by the enemy's evil hands, pitifully and alone.

Sister Peter was a sturdy practical woman. Her honest face had seen some forty-five summers. She was not given to frothy emotion. Even now her hand did not waver as the ancient Korean characters flowed from her modern ball-point pen. But tears rolled one by one over her cheeks and dropped from the dark skinned jowls.

My venerable Mother General! I have written too little about my Mother in this not-so-short letter. Your daughter Sister Agneta's virtuousness was far advanced. The old, the young and even all the children in the district were happy at the mere mention of her. To everyone, she was everything, and to all us nuns she was an ideal model. She not only loved to give, but always gave her best. Her love for us was sympathetic.

Is there another person who had such devotion for her own Maryknoll order or respected her Mother General as she did? Was there ever one who loved us, her younger Sisters, as she did? Between these two objects of her love, she has risen to the world of eternity. I can only think that she has knotted us eternally with you who gave her to us, upon one and the same cord.

8

Operation: Small Fry

"Blue Heaven" opened on November 15th.

It was a pre-fab building twenty by sixty feet long. Servicemen, working on their free time, spent many weeks in putting it up. The Children's Clinic, heretofore crowded into one small room, expanded now into three examination cubicles, a room for minor surgery, treatment rooms, a pharmacy and a small office. Just outside the main entrance, the walls of a large Army tent bellied in a stiff November wind. It served as waiting room for the thousand or more children who daily passed through the Clinic's treatment rooms.

The name "Blue Heaven"? Oh, when the building was painted there was nothing but blue paint available, so the outside looked like a glimpse of sky through the trees. By the time the inside was ready for paint, white was available. Walls and partitions were gay with pictures—children and animals cut from old magazines.

Marvellous people came to Blue Heaven. Heavenly people, such as Doctors Stryker and Burkle who gave long hours to work on small tuberculous hips and spines and arms and legs; such as the old woman, dressed in rags, pressing money into Sister's hand as she said, "No, this is not to pay for my medicine. Use it to buy food for somebody poorer than I"; such as Chung On breaking her chocolate bar into three parts so that her little sisters at home could have a bite, too. Funny things happened there, such as the thank-you speech of a nervous lad who was all set to present Sister Augusta with an apple. Mama coached his presentation speech from the side lines. "I have two very kind old grandmothers," he said. "A one grandmother is at home and a one grandmother is here, which grandmother is yourself."

Heavenly, too, was the law and order. Sister Dolorosa and three assistants put a new system into effect so that everyone was tended to in order and received medicines without having to crowd around the pharmacy window.

"Sister M.P.," the service boys called Sister Dolorosa. She took it in good humor but kept a watchful eye, nonetheless, on maintaining the peace.

All too many children used Blue Heaven as a jumping-off place for a far happier heaven. But others came back again and again, each time a little heavier to carry, a little rosier, a lot livelier. These were the "Peanut Butter Babies."

Sister Agnus Therese writes home:

> *Having been out of the running with hepatitis for a few weeks, I can see now how medicine and food are transforming many of our little skeletons. Yesterday Sister Mercy called me in to see a boy of seven smiling and in fairly good nutrition. Then she showed me the admission card where I had written a couple of months ago, "Skin and Bones." Food and vitamins have surely made a new boy of him.*
>
> *There is Helen, too, now about nine months old. Not so long ago she was a favorite subject for our visitors' cameras because she was extremely emaciated but always friendly. Now she is almost chubby—and still friendly in spite of all the injections.*
>
> *You should see Chung Tsa, alias The Chocolate Bar Kid! Five months ago, this four-year-old was extremely malnour-*

ished, a little skeleton too weak to walk. Now she has a fat round face and even a double chin. We feed her chocolate bars every time she comes to the clinic—and does she like them! Her two hands reach out to take them every time we hold them out to her.

But each day still brings us new little waifs at death's door. The first one I saw this morning was a little girl of four whose blood is like water. Not a tint of pink in her lips or nails. Listless, of course. Hookworms have literally sucked out all her blood. A transfusion is her immediate need and we are trying to get some blood for her. After getting rid of the hookworms, iron and vitamins should restore her to health.

The next will not be easily cured; I fear there are only a few days left for him. He is a three-year-old boy, extremely emaciated with a chest full of tuberculosis. His mother died from starvation; his father is at the battle front. The dear old grandmother is deeply devoted to him. The child is a pitiful sight, just able to whimper. His pathetic brown eyes look so large in his sunken face.

Some of "the world's sickest babies" (as newspapermen said) came to Blue Heaven. Also—according to Sister Augusta—some of the world's best squallers.

Pok Dong, aged two, could scream an octave higher and at least three stops louder than anyone else. Perched high on his mother's back one morning, he used his powers to the full. Sister Augusta's usual treatment was to stick a lollypop into the wide-open mouth and await the cease-fire.

When she reached over to the lollypop supply, however, there wasn't another one left. And just yesterday a generous soldier-boy had brought three hundred! Well, she had known those would not last the morning out.

Pok Dong must have known too. He screamed when his mother sat him down on the treatment table. He yelled when Sister uncovered his little buttocks to find a place for the injection. He all but burst a blood vessel when she came near with the needle poised in her hand. "This has got to stop," Sister told herself, "if only to preserve sanity in the rest of us."

She ducked away from the crowd for a minute and slipped into Sister Herman Joseph's laboratory. If ever you want a glimpse of never-never land you should see that laboratory. "A cross between Betty Crocker's Kitchen and Sol's Bargain Basement," they called it. The laboratory part was immaculate— instruments gleaming, microscopes and scales in perfect order. The rest was—until a separate room could be constructed—a welter of clothes, food cartons, barrels of powdered milk, old magazines and Christmas cards. At that particular moment, too, an old man and a boy were lying side by side on the floor behind some cartons. This was a familiar enough sight. Often patients had to rest before setting out for home again. Sister Herman Joseph's room, though confused, was always immaculate. A quiet nap behind some cartons would do the trick for many a patient.

"Quick!" Sister Augusta called to Sister Herman Joseph, who was just then bending over a slide in the microscope. "I need a peace offering."

"Why don't you try peanut butter?" Sister Herman Joseph said without looking up. "There's a carton of it right beside you."

Pok Dong would have none of it at first. He was right in the middle of a good bawl and did not want to be interrupted. Sister Augusta with a firm hand took his finger and scooped up a mouthful of peanut butter from the jar. Quick as a wink she inserted the finger loaded with brown stuff into the large cavity which produced the noise. Like a bear trap, Pok Dong closed down. And stayed closed down. His next sound was a low gurgle of content.

Grinning at Sister between each fingerful, the ex-noisemaker took everything in cheerful stride. The injection, the thermometer, the treatment of an abscess, were mere incidentals between further helpings of peanut butter. When last seen, he was

99

strapped to his mother's back with the jar firmly clutched right within finger range.

Sister Herman Joseph's relief work was one of the greatest sagas of the clinic. She helped thousands of people and had a grand time doing it. Anybody who helped her to help the thousands enjoyed the experience thoroughly.

Sometimes the people didn't know just what they were getting into. The rule in the clinic was to send to Sister Herman Joseph anyone who looked as if he needed warm clothes. Shivering little tots with teeth chattering would creep into the laboratory expecting to get anything from a major operation to a bill for services rendered.

One woman was sent in by Sister Magdalena. Now Sister Magdalena was newly come to Korea after fifteen years in South China. The intricacies of Korean grammar were a little too much for her. She did what she could, with her Chinese-Korean eked out with plenty of gestures. In the Clinic one morning, giving injections like wildfire, she shoved up a flimsy cotton sleeve and thrust the needle into a wrinkled arm which was almost blue with cold. "Go in there," she said, pulling down the sleeve and pointing over to the laboratory. The poor old soul started off to follow the crowd now going out the middle door, but Sister Magdalena took her out of line and escorted her personally to the laboratory. "Right here," she said, opening the door and starting her through it. Then she returned to the crowd awaiting injections.

Old Nam Sin didn't know what was happening to her. She continued through the door. Trembling with anxiety as much as with cold, she sat herself on a carton near the door. Sister Herman Joseph hardly noticed her; she was busy tallying up a blood test needed immediately. When she did look, ready to turn her attention to Nam Sin, the old lady leaped to her feet saying,

"A thousands pardons for misbehaving! I'm sure I meant nothing wrong, honorable *Su Nyo*."

What a relief when Sister explained in Korean that Nam Sin

was in for—not a correction—but a beautiful suit of warm clothes!

Sometimes Sister Herman Joseph's bargain basement was stocked with everything from ballgowns to ski pants. All of it came from the generous people here, there and everywhere. The Swedish doctor and nurse got their friends back home to send crates of warm clothes from Sweden. Much of the clothing came from Thanksgiving collections throughout the States, in the Bishop's Drive, and channeled through NCWC Catholic Relief Services. Mother Aurelia, Mother General of the St. Joseph Sisters in Erie, Pennsylvania, personally went from store to store in town getting brand new shirts for men.

Even Hawaii, a little at a loss for winter things, contributed cases of clothing. Pictures show the Koreans exulting in colorful Aloha shirts, loud enough to be heard above Pok Dong's powerful bellows.

Most needed of all were the layettes for babies. Surely the Christ Child Himself was outdone in poverty as these innocents came into the world without even swaddling clothes to wear or a manger of hay to lie in.

JANUARY 15. *Freezing winds have been blowing in from the Pacific for the past few days. They bring untold suffering to our thousands. Many tents around the city—homes for hundreds— have collapsed, or they have burned down when stoves inside set fire to the cloth.*

We came across two young mothers who expect their babies in a matter of days. One lives in a cardboard box at present. The other is simply on the street since her tent was blown down. They were so grateful for the warm clothing we gave them and for the layettes Sister Herman Joseph has ready for expectant mothers. Best of all were the comforters our Korean Sisters have made for them.

The comforters were a bright idea of Sister Mercy's. With

donations tagged for charity, she bought a great deal of cotton. The Korean Sisters made the comforters and also knitted sweaters from bright yarn sent in by donors. This provided a living for the Sisters who could not work in the Marine laundry or do active duty about the Clinic.

Koreans don't know any more about the right way to wear our clothes than we know about wearing theirs. I remember once at school we were in a Japanese play, togged out in beautiful Japanese kimonos of lovely pastel shades. When we children came off stage, flushed with achievement, we were greeted by a horrified Japanese woman expostulating to the director.

"But Sister!" she said, "You can't have them walking around in those kimonos! That's only our underwear!"

Similarly, Sister Herman Joseph had a good laugh to herself when she saw Mun Ki Poong proudly strutting around in the crowd clad in a bright red flannelette sleeping suit complete right down to the built-in foot warmers. In sartorial elegance, he knew he was tops.

When she had money, Sister Herman Joseph sometimes went into the loan business, strictly on a non-profit basis, of course. One of her best investments was the fifty cents given to Byung No, business man, aged eight.

He was skinny and ragged, but resolute.

"I want to see the *Su Nyo,*" he announced to Frances Register who was taking care of "clothes line" one day.

"Right over there, young man." Frances pointed to Sister Herman Joseph working at the microscope.

She recognized Byung No. Sister Agnus Therese had found the family in a cardboard hut. Just the father and the two boys were left. The mother had died of cold and exhaustion on the road; the baby sister had withered away. They needed food and clothes desperately. Byung No appeared twice a week in the line to get a regular supply. He was an old customer.

"What's on your mind?" Sister asked him.

The boy screwed up his courage. "I—I—have come to borrow money from you," he blurted out.

Sister put down her pencil and turned to him.

"What for?"

"I'm going into business and I need money to start with."

"What kind of business, Byung No?"

"Selling water. I will carry water to people who will pay me for it."

"Oh no, Byung No!" Sister said, taking his frail little shoulders between her hands. "You're not strong enough to carry those five-gallon gasoline tins. That's man's work. If you need food...."

The boy broke in. "I won't carry the big buckets, Sister. That's my idea. On our hill many people like us cannot afford 25 hwaun for water. I can sell them smaller buckets for 15 hwaun. Please Sister, you know my father can't work yet. I'm sure I can make money."

"How much do you need to start with?" Sister asked.

Byung No drew in his breath. How could he even name such a fortune? "Well, you see, I have to buy two small buckets and a shoulder pole. Can you lend me . . . fifty cents?"

The deal was made. And within ten days Byung No repaid the loan. He had a nice little business set up with regular customers. The family still needed help, of course, but Byung No felt himself no longer strictly "on the dole." It's a good feeling to have.

In *West Coast Sailors,* a seamen's newssheet published by the Sailors' Union of the Pacific, Charlie Goldsmith wrote:

The Old Man was looking pretty serious as we came into the messroom for coffee yesterday morning. Yep, all of us boys in the deck crew of the SS *New Zealand Victory* didn't know what to expect from the Old Man. He just sat waiting for every deck hand to get into the messroom. Then he opened up.

"Boys," he said, "I have a little story to tell you. A sad story, but I'm sure we can help to brighten it some anyway.

"As you know, some of you have been complaining about weevils in the cereal. Yesterday, I went down into the storeroom to examine the stuff. Yes indeed, some thirty pounds of various cereals were badly infested with weevils. We condemned it.

"I ordered the steward to bring it up on deck so that it could be dumped overboard when we got outside the harbor here at Pusan. When Mr. Giesa of the National Seaman's Association heard me tell the steward that he piped up.

" 'Hey, Cap. Don't do that,' he said. 'Don't you know about the Maryknoll Sisters' Clinic?'

" 'No, I don't,' I said. 'What about it?'

" 'It's run by the Catholic Sisters to help the poor. If you give that cereal to me, I'll take it up there and they will use it to feed the babies.'

" 'Well, answer me this,' I told him. 'How in the world can they use it to feed babies when I have just condemned it as unfit for human consumption?'

" 'You don't know those Sisters, Cap,' he told me. 'They will sit up all night if necessary and pick out every weevil by hand.'

"Well, I said it was okay to take the stuff up to the Clinic. And Mr. Giesa invited me to come along and see what it was all about.

"Boys, I went along. And I saw enough misery and human suffering to last me forever.

"You should have seen the baby clinic. Outside, waiting their turn, stood young mothers in their twenties looking like they were sixty. I saw children and babies; consumptive children; children suffering from every imaginable disease, all of which are caused by starvation.

"In this Clinic, they treat from eleven hundred to twelve hundred patients a day, nearly 500,000 a year. It's hard to believe, but it is so."

The Old Man stopped a minute. I've never seen him so worked up about anything.

"Now I'm not a Catholic," he went on, "and I don't believe many of us on this ship are. But church affiliation doesn't matter. The Maryknoll Sisters don't ask the poor, the sick and the starving whether they are Buddhist, Catholic or Protestant. They just open their hearts and treat them all alike. And boys, they do it with a smile.

"I asked what we could do to help them and the head Sister said old clothing would be useful. In fact, they would use anything.

"You men go down and search your lockers for clothing you can

104

give. And look in your pockets, too, for any green stuff you can get along without."

That was some story the Captain told us. If it was only half as bad as he said, it must be pretty bad. So I made a motion for each of us to donate five bucks. It was passed unanimously.

We got busy on the old clothes and gathered up a laundry bag full of stuff. It had to be in darn good shape to qualify, too. We took it and the $75 from the deck gang up to the Old Man's room.

He already had a big pile of stuff from the other crews, and the "green stuff" was coming in as well. Altogether he had collected $168 in greenbacks, and a little over $30 in yen for a total of $200.00. As for the clothing, our laundry bag plus five big boxes from the rest of the men on board, was collected.

When this stuff was taken up to the Clinic I went along for the ride. The skipper hadn't exaggerated a thing, I decided. Conditions were even worse than he said.

What I'm writing this piece in the paper for is to suggest that all ships coming to Pusan gather up their bundles of old clothing and give it to the Maryknoll Sisters' Clinic. And don't forget the green stuff either!

The Sisters wrote us a real nice letter of thanks. They said, "I think you would have loved to see the smile of joy and surprise lighting the faces of these people as they received your help. Many of the youngsters are little skeletons. But it is a joy to see them brighten up and put on weight with the aid of vitamins and milk, peanut butter, and cereal."

Boys, I want to tell you that aboard the *New Zealand Victory*, the faces of us tough seamen have brightened up, too.

Now we will have to go behind the scenes. How did Sister Herman Joseph, busy at her laboratory work, find time to run a relief station as well? There is so much to be done besides the mere handing out of food and clothes. Packaging, arranging, storing—how was that done? Ah, this was the work of her Fifth Column, her band of conscriptees, her Child Labor workers. In a word, the "Our Gang" of Pusan. They were her devoted slaves!

Sister Herman Joseph is one of those people who can do anything. Build a house? Knit a sweater? Take a jeep apart? Grow African violets? They were all as simple to her as counting the bacteria in a slide or keeping track of the frequency of tuberculosis among Korean refugees. She threw her whole mind and heart into any work set before her.

Small wonder! As Mary Dorchen Stitz of Salem, Oregon, she had to turn her hand to anything and everything. There were seven girls in the family; they had to learn to work together—or else.

All of this was good training for Maryknoll in 1930. For when Mary Dorchen Stitz became Sister Herman Joseph, the Maryknoll Sisters were living in three farmhouses, a barn, an ex-carriage house, and an assortment of attics. They bundled up and walked through the snow from building to building following the day's schedule—Mass, meals, chapel exercises, work and, finally, bed.

Her mission years were strictly for pioneers, too. She proved her versatility during five years in Korea and three in Shanghai as well as several in the Philippines. She spent nearly a year as prisoner of war and returned to the United States on a repatriation ship in 1942. When she returned to Korea, she was part of the medical team under Sister Mercy. It was the kind of life in which one had to be resourceful.

No one ever thinks of Sister Herman Joseph as exclusively a medical technician, although she is a very good one. Rather, they remember a short, squarish, warm-hearted person, very practical, tingling with ideas how to get things done in the best possible way and the shortest possible time.

So it was that she commanded her faithful little army, Our Gang. By this time the Clinic had many employees. There were the gateman, the night watchman, the carpenter, the jeep driver, the kitchen man, the general handyman, etc. They and their families lived here and there about the place, often in small houses built from packing cases. All together, with wives and children they made a colony of about sixty people.

The children were underfoot everywhere at first. Then, Sister Herman Joseph became Officer of the Day for them every day.

The first big job was the utilization of the Matzos cases. Forty huge wooden crates were stacked in the yard. Nobody had the time to dismantle them and get out the precious food for Pusan's starving poor. But not for long. Sister Herman Joseph organized Our Gang.

Sister André writes home to Covington, Kentucky:

What a picture they are! The boys are perched high on the piles of boxes, the girls at lower heights, all engaged in removing the wrappers from the Matzos boxes.

"Don't tear the paper," Sister Herman Joseph just called out from the laboratory window. "We'll need it for wrapping other things." You should see how carefully the youngsters smooth out the papers and pile them off to one side.

Ten-year-old Francis, the gateman's son, is the oldest. His sister Clara is the youngest. She is three and the apple of her father's eye. There are about a dozen in all, doing their good deed for the day and enjoying it hugely.

Their reward? Why, Matzos, of course! Also red, white and blue T shirts for the boys and overalls in the same colors for the girls. Pusan's Our Gang will be looking like a long line of Old Glory, lined up at the front gate this evening as Father Rush bids farewell.

Father is, you might say, our oldest and best Army friend here. As Chief of Chaplains he has been instrumental in all sorts of aid. He is always directing the boys to come over here and see for themselves. Through him, the boys have become so interested that they have contributed enough money to buy the property here for the Clinic.

This evening, Our Gang will do a few simple dances and impromptu recitations and songs for Father. Then they will sing—I can hear it now!—the Korean National Anthem, sounding it from the deepest recesses of their young lungs.

Very appropriate, I would say. It will be the children of Pusan thanking Father for all he has done to help the sick little children of Korea.

Trained on the Matzos, Our Gang next went to work on the pill situation. With a daily average of a thousand patients, it was next to impossible to keep on the shelves little bags of routine medicines, ready to hand out quickly. Some eight to ten thousand vitamin pills alone were given out in a single day. Thirteen hundred prescriptions were filled daily.

It was Sister Alberta Marie who supervised this pill squad. A regular assembly line technique evolved. Big boys cut sealed envelopes in half to make small cup-like bags. The older girls, eight and ten years old, counted out twelve pills. The next girl checked the number and put them in a bag. Then four-year-old Annie and three-year-old Clara carefully folded down the corners so that the pills would not fall out.

Tommy, at two and a half, felt he ought to fit into this new game some way, but he soon lost interest and turned in his card, so to speak, seeking more fascinating employment elsewhere. But when Sister Alberta Marie, as paymaster, handed each child a small box of hard candy, Tommy was right in line. Unlike the laborers in the Gospel, the other children who had borne the heat of the day insisted that Tommy be given full wages for his "eleventh hour."

Just a few days later came the barrels of powdered milk and eggs from the Civil Assistance Command. Sister Agnus Therese beamed with delight. How wonderful it would be, for instance, for three-year-old Maria, whom she was visiting up on the mountain side. Just a short time before, the old grandmother had beckoned Sister into her shanty. With a gesture more eloquent than words she pointed to the shrunken little figure lying on a heap of rags in the corner.

Even before making the least medical examination, Sister Agnus Therese dropped on her knees and taking the little vial of water from her bag, she named another Maria for the heavenly court. She was sure the child would be there shortly. However, she happened to have some blood plasma with her and gave Maria some. Two more pints followed later and relief supplies for Grandma. Today, the old woman brought Maria to the Clinic. Coming along very well indeed! Milk and eggs would keep right on putting her out of reach when Death stretched his claw out for her.

It's fine to have barrels of milk and eggs, but how to get it to the people? Our Gang to the rescue!

Out came the waxed paper wrappers saved from the Matzos boxes. Out came three cups for the oldest, Francis, Kum Ah and Kap Sugie. Out came the large cartons where the filled bags would be stored. And out came the Generalissimo, Sister Herman Joseph.

"Ready, men?" said the Commanding Officer.

"Ready, Sir."

"Oh yes? Let me see your hands!"

The pudgy paws went up for inspection.

"Out to the faucet you go! It's right outside the laboratory and the soap is alongside."

The troops did a double-quick out and back.

"Good!" said Sister Herman Joseph. "Now we begin."

Such fun! Open a bag—and pass it on. Put four cupfuls into it—and pass it on. Fold down the top—and pass it on. Place the filled bags in the carton—and let them stay!

Tommy was the villain again. When he wasn't getting into everybody's way, he was off in the corner poking holes into filled bags. He wedged himself between the barrels and had to be pulled out by a G.I. Francis was all for letting him stay wedged. At least, you could keep your eye on him there; you knew where he was. But Tommy won by sheer lung power. After that the Generalissimo marched him off to the laboratory and let him play with the toy pussy cat he wasn't supposed to see until Christmas.

Our Gang had an even better time cleaning up. With buckets of water they sloshed all over the porch floor, sliding in their bare feet on the slippery surface. Then they dried it off—and heaven help anybody who walked across that floor! Bishop Ro of Seoul, who had been visiting upstairs, came by. He was graciously allowed to pass, but Sister Agnus Therese was stopped at the border and equipped with rags on her feet lest she mar that gleaming surface.

What a morning! Our Gang ganged up on their Generalissimo. They volunteered to play hookey from school if she wanted them to work that afternoon, too. But she marched them of to class instead.

From then on, the small fry were often called upon for emergencies. They wrapped yeast powder into small portions when the vitamin pill supply ran out and yeast powder was substituted. They did a grand job with the peanut butter. For this, the "Special Service Squad," as they called themselves after hearing a service man say it, was ranged around a big packing case. They were to transfer the spread from #10 tin cans to small waxed containers.

"Try to be quiet," the Generalissimo cautioned, pointing to a curtain behind them. "The Korean Sisters are working just on the other side of that. If you make too much noise, you'll disturb them."

The Generalissimo herself didn't believe it would have much effect. But an hour later she found them plugging away in absolute silence. They looked up, smiled, waved peanut-buttery hands—and said nothing.

At the end of the morning the troops, still on good behavior, tip-toed up to the laboratory window, turned to salute the High Command, and went screaming off to lunch.

With an eye to the future, Sister Herman Joseph collected a number of dull scissors and set her battalion to cutting pictures from old magazines. Even Tommy could tear up bright paper into good-ish squares, or circles, or triangles. "What for?" they wanted to know. "You'll see!" was all the satisfaction she gave them.

Next, they had to put loops of bright cord through the pictures and string the bits of paper on a thread. Awfully funny! thought Francis.

On December 22nd, the mystery cleared. A Jewish lad struggled up the stairway carrying a big Christmas tree. A sign on it said, "To Our Gang, from Benny." All those pretty pictures and all that colored paper were soon strung from bough to bough. Benny concocted Christmas tree lights from a length of electric wire and bulbs painted different colors. Frances Register had made reflectors for the bulbs.

Now, to place the star on the very tip-top! Sister Alberta Marie was in a pretty fix. She had a ladder all right, but everyone was too busy to hold it for her while she climbed to the top. She was looking around helplessly when two American civilians came to the rescue. They peeled off their coats and scaled to the top. Only then did Sister recognize them as important wheels in the American embassy from Seoul.

Our Gang were enchanted as the evening grew dark and their very own Christmas tree stood forth in all its glory.

It was, perhaps, the only outdoor Christmas tree in Pusan that year. Set high on the mountains, it could be seen from far out in the harbor.

"Men on the ships," said Sister André, "can look up on our hill and find a wee bit of home there. And that in itself is a very special kind of relief work."

9

Much in a Short Time

On her knees, Frances Register thanked God for the year almost past. And for Christmas just beginning.

She had slipped into chapel after the strenuous day to spend the last hour or so of Christmas Eve talking to Our Lady and her Divine Son. What was the use of going back to the old "21st Evac." only to return so soon for Midnight Mass?

In her dark corner, she let her tired body relax. She and a number of other nurses had made up 1,000 little bags of cookies and candy; today they gave them out to the children attending the clinic. It was seven when the last little tyke went out the door on Mamma's back, the precious bag clutched in a chubby hand.

The others had gone home early in the evening, but Frances stayed around helping to fix the chapel, getting things wrapped for Sister Mercy to give the Korean help, making herself useful in a thousand ways.

Now was the lull. The Maryknoll Sisters were getting in a few hours rest. Only the Sister-sacristan moved quietly in the dim light near the sanctuary putting last minute touches to preparations for a High Mass. Frances could speak quietly and intimately to God.

"Thanks for this year," she said almost aloud. "I've never been so tired. I've never worked so hard. I've never been so completely used by others. I've never had so little for myself.

I've never been so absolutely happy. Thank you! Thank you!"

Was it just last March that she and Catherine Little had knocked on the door asking permission to gather flowers from the overrun garden? Well, if the Japanese gentleman who planted the garden could see the place now, he would never recognize it.

Blue Heaven was set near the old wisteria arbor. Occupied only six weeks, it was already too small to handle the crowds. Work was starting on a two-story Children's Clinic, much bigger, to be built right beside Blue Heaven. The waiting shed, the Army tent, the new wing for the laboratory, the tent where every Wednesday orthopods from hospital ships put some thirty-five children into casts—these were placed here and there through the once-palatial garden. High up on the mountain near the top of the property was a new little convent built for the Korean Sisters. Other small but neat houses had sprung up like mushrooms as homes for the Korean help.

Only this chapel building, the exquisite Japanese home, was pretty much as Nakamura San had built it. Frances' eyes traveled over the simple altar and backdrape set against one side of the large room. "Poor man," she murmured. "He had this lovely home and never knew that God would live in it."

There was talk now about making a driveway into the property. This would mean taking down the stairway which led to the street and grading a steep slope up from the street.

"I've seen it all happen, dear Lord," Frances told Him. "I've spent some part of each day here doing something to further the work. Thank you for that privilege."

There was no part of the work in which Frances had not helped. She painted furniture, bathed and dressed the refugees, visited the sick in their homes and spent many long hours in nursing. Besides, she had brought other nurses and even doctors to give their free time to the Clinic. Every day had brought her willing hands and cheerful smile to ease the work load on the Sisters.

How many more days? There couldn't be many. Her term

of service was running out. Probably she would go back to the States in February. Many of the Clinic helpers were going. Mignon Johnson, the Navy nurse from the hospital ship *Repose*, was to go on January 15th. Father Rush, Chief of Chaplains, had gone already.

Constantly shifting personnel! She was not worried, however. It was God's work. He would send somebody to take her place.

Out in the dark night music began. Christmas carols! Frances remembered that this was a Maryknoll custom—to sing carols rather than ring a prosaic bell to wake the Sisters for Midnight Mass. Here, with only nine Sisters, the four youngest were waking up the other five.

The voices swelled and dimmed in the crisp air as the singers trailed around the grounds. Frances could recognize the voices —there was Sister Agnus Therese, steady and clear, and Sister Rose of Lima's fine voice. They led the group. Sister Herman Joseph provided volume. Sister Alberta Marie blended in with them all.

"That was Sister all over," Frances thought. "She blends in. And that's so important for a Nun. I wonder, if I were a Sister like Sister Alberta Marie, would I blend in, too?"

Not entirely a theoretical question. Frances Register and Sister Alberta Marie were just about the same age—twenty-six. When Frances was a freshman in nursing school, Alberta Hanley bade farewell to her parents in Detroit and entered the convent at Maryknoll, New York. She came from a prominent family in Detroit. Her father and brother had graduated from Harvard. "Odd, that Sister herself studied at Yale," Frances thought.

Frances took her diploma in nursing just when Sister Alberta Marie pronounced her vows. "She must have been very deliberate about it," Frances said to herself. "I don't suppose she ever says anything she absolutely does not mean. At twenty-one, she definitely gave her life to God to use for His own purposes."

And what would be His purposes? How would He use the life of this young Sister? She was a teacher. Perhaps when time

became settled she would start educational work here in Korea
—a Maryknoll School like those in Hong Kong and Kowloon
and Manila, or in other Philippine towns. Maybe she would go
from village to village in Korea as the Sisters do in Japan. The
Sisters from China, Sister Magdalena and Sister Dolorosa, talked
of that kind of work in China before the Communist government expelled them.

"Here I am settling the future for her!" Frances smiled to
herself. "Let's face it. I haven't the faintest notion what God
has up His sleeve for her. She doesn't either. Nobody does. I
wonder what I'll be doing ten years from now!"

People were coming into chapel now. Koreans in their gaily
striped sleeves, which are reserved for very special occasions.
They knelt down quietly on the floor and sat back gently on
their heels. The Korean Sisters did the same; they were more
comfortable that way. The Maryknoll Sisters, being stiff-jointed
Americans, had to have chairs and prie-dieux. Only two other
Army people besides Frances were invited—Major Breyfogle of
the Medical Supply Depot, and Sergeant Hull whose untiring
energy had laid the chapel floor.

Guests of honor for the evening were seventeen men and
women seated in flowing white up in front. They were the
neophytes who had been baptized just that morning. Tonight,
in their hearts, they would receive the Lord of Lords, the King
of Kings, God Almighty, the Babe of Bethlehem.

Eleven-thirty! A gong sounded in the back of the chapel. The
Sisters stood and in two choirs faced each other across the room.

A high clear voice rang out.

"Incline unto mine aid, O God."

"Oh Lord, hasten to help me!" the Sisters responded in
volume. Thus started the Divine Office for Christmas Day.

The chanting continued on, sometimes one lone voice, then
another, then the whole choir. Sometimes the right side of
chapel called to the left, and the left responded in glad phrases.
Occasionally two Sisters left their places and met in the middle

of the center aisle. They chanted, bowed to each other and returned.

Frances, who knew them all so well felt now that she knew them not at all. Was this meek nun with bowed head and book clasped in both hands like a medieval figure—was she the same Sister André of the quick-typing fingers, the bookkeeping ledgers, the decisions of where to pile this stuff and how to put that complicated adding machine into working order? Surely it was not Sister Rose of Lima, the pharmacist, and Sister Augusta, the nurse, who stepped sedately from their places, met in the aisle, bowed to each other, chanted a verse or so, bowed again and returned to their seats! And Sister Mercy sitting there as impersonal as a statue! Who would suppose that her delicate hands had examined hundreds of sick bodies that very day? Who could suspect that in her head, bowed now at the Gloria, was crammed medical knowledge and experience many a physician in the States might envy?

"This is their double life," Frances concluded. "I've known only half so far. This is where they get their stamina and courage. This is the repose which generates their tremendous activity."

Twelve! The clock bonged interminably. With the last stroke still quivering, Monsignor Carroll of Maryknoll, Acting Apostolic Delegate to Korea since Bishop Byrne had been taken prisoner from Seoul, entered the sanctuary. Midnight Mass began.

Frances wrote home later,

> "We were packed so tightly in that chapel that Major Breyfogle and I could easily read the same missal. He is a recent convert and it was his first High Mass. I'm not used to High Masses, either.
>
> Neither of us knew when to stand or kneel. We tried to watch the Sisters but could hardly turn enough to see them.
>
> Mass had just started when Ye Olde Pusan Electricity went off. A good thing, too. It was a beautiful service in that very plain little chapel by candlelight. I'll never forget it!"

Soft black mud underfoot; clear sky overhead. Such was the setting for Cardinal Spellman's visit on December 28th. With him were General Van Fleet, chief of the UN Forces here in Korea, General Yount and other high Army officers. We did our best to show off our place but it must have seemed a very humble compound at best. Anyway, as the important visitors stood in the room which we hope will be a laboratory some day, His Eminence looked around at the bareness of it all.

"What did you say this is to be?" he asked Sister Mercy.

"A laboratory, we hope, Your Eminence."

"Hmmm. How much do you think it will cost to equip a laboratory?"

Sister Mercy hesitated. She knew he must be contemplating a gift and she hesitated to make it too high. $1,000? No, better make it $500.

Sister Herman Joseph had no such qualms. After all, a technician could not see a fine laboratory go by for want of asking for it.

"$5,000, Your Eminence."

Sister Mercy gasped. The Cardinal must have many demands on his charity. They shouldn't. . . .

His Eminence laughed. "Good! Who has a pen I can borrow?"

Half a dozen pens shot toward him. He took one and wrote a figure on a blank check. Then he gave it to Sister Mercy. She nearly dropped in a faint. It was for $10,000, a gift from the Knights of Malta through Cardinal Spellman.

Language! Or rather, languages! Swedish nurse and Danish doctor, Korean patients and American servicemen, British visitors and Norwegian corpsmen. And now we take on the Chinese as well!

This morning a Chinese woman came up to Sister Augusta and said that she lives in a village not far away which has a large Chinese population. They have heard of the Clinic, but they thought it is meant only for Koreans. "May Chinese people also be treated here?" she asked.

Assured that they would be most welcome, the woman returned home. This afternoon she brought three other Chinese women, all in need of medical care. Luckily, Sister Augusta, Sister Magdalena and Sister Dolorosa all speak Chinese fluently. We don't know who were happier—the Sisters or the women—as they chattered gaily in an old familiar language.

There are others in the town, too, who will be coming in. They are overjoyed to know that three of us here will be able to talk to them in their own tongue.

We can appreciate what a cross the Tower of Babel was to our high-building ancestors! Two Okinawan women came to us with a very sick baby. The mother spoke only Okinawan; her friend knew a little Japanese as well. A chain of languages was strung across the abyss of incomprehension, so that the doctor could contact her small patient. The mother spoke in Okinawan to her friend. The friend repeated it in Japanese to a Korean Sister. The Sister translated it into Korean for Sister Agnus Therese. Sister then made the diagnosis, wrote out the history and prescription in English, translated it again into Korean for the native Sister to put into Japanese so that the friend could tell it in Okinawan to the mother. We hope the baby lives!

THURSDAY, JANUARY 24. They were at recreation, sitting around the tiny community room doing odds and ends and chatting.

"Where's Sister Alberta Marie?" someone asked.

"She's tired and I told her to go to bed early," Sister Mercy responded.

"She has been tired for several days," Sister Rose of Lima put in. "I've noticed it in the pharmacy. . . . I'm glad she's taking extra rest."

"Look!" It was Sister Alberta Marie herself laughing in the doorway. "Look how funny my arms are. Did you ever see such a speckled herring?"

The two doctors leaped up from their easy chairs. Arms, legs, neck and body were covered with hemorrhages under the skin.

Even her gums were bleeding. Blood was in her nose and throat as well.

"I've had a nosebleed all day," she said, "but it's nothing serious."

The two doctors looked at each other.

"Thrombocytopoenia?" asked Sister Agnus Therese.

"I'm afraid so," said Sister Mercy.

Sister Herman Joseph ran down to her laboratory with a small sample of blood. The blood platelets were greatly reduced; this had caused the hemorrhages. Yes, thrombocytopoenia probably.

That same night, Sister Alberta Marie entered the 21st Evacuation Hospital. The personnel here knew the Maryknollers very well. Besides Frances Register and a host of the nurses, there was Doctor Barbaro who spent hours at the clinic. Just two days before, the servicemen and women of the "21st Evac." had sent a beautiful binocular microscope for the laboratory with this note:

"We wish to show our appreciation of the wonderful work you are doing for the glory of God.

"Perhaps this instrument will indicate in a slight way how wonderful we think your work is."

Dr. Barbaro, ever faithful, had secured a room in the private section. "I must say, young lady," he bantered, "you choose good company! Ambassador Muccio, a general, and a couple of colonels are on the same floor. VIP's only in your section! You have a VIP illness, too. Thrombocytopoenia is a rare disorder of the spleen and other blood-making organs. Now you can write home all about your interesting disease. Oh, don't be frightened; you'll get as good care as you could anywhere in the world. The Chief Surgeon of the Far East Command is on his way here now and we'll have a consultation. I don't know how you do it, my dear, but you certainly rate as top brass!"

But his shoulders sagged as he closed the door behind him and faced Sister Mercy and Sister Rose of Lima in the hall.

"You know what it means, I suppose."

"Yes," they said. "We know."

SUNDAY, JANUARY 27. "Good news!" beamed the M.P. at the hospital gate as Sister Mercy hurried through at noon.

"Yes?"

"A nurse told me. She said one of the M.D.'s on Sister's case dashed into the Mess Hall waving laboratory reports in his hand. 'Sister's blood has picked up,' he announced, and got a real salvo of applause."

"Thanks ever so much for the news. It means a lot that everybody makes us feel so welcome," and the grey habit passed quickly in.

Sister Alberta Marie was happy but quiet.

"It looks as if I'm really going to get better," she said slowly. "And after I had placed myself so securely at peace in God's hands! It will be strange and different now to come back when I thought I was going to die."

"I had an experience once like that," Sister Mercy said.

The young nun smiled as she lay back on the pillows, a soft white veil replacing the stiff black one she usually wore. She squeezed Sister Mercy's hand.

"And see what God has let you do for Him since!"

THURSDAY, JANUARY 31. "Not so good," muttered the M.P. as the two figures in grey hurried through the hospital door. "Took a turn for the worse last night."

She was very still on the pillows now, but she turned to smile a welcome. "Did you hear the report, Sister?" she asked. "I'm going back on you now. But I'm very happy. I feel just like a child in God's hands."

Sister Mercy planned to spend the night there. Doctors said she would linger for several days, but Sister Mercy looked with more than a doctor's insight. The loving mother, the good Superior in her, felt that time was very short indeed.

"Frances Register is on duty here," she told the Sisters. "I'll call you all if she gets any worse."

Seven o'clock.

Eight o'clock.

Nine o'clock.

"My head," said the quiet voice. "I feel as though it is tied in a tight, tight band. Round and round."

Sister Mercy bent over and whispered.

"Our Lord's crown of thorns must have felt something like that."

A small smile crept to the corners of the still mouth.

"Yes," she said. "Something like this."

She could not see now, for the blood was seeping into her eyeballs. Sister Mercy placed an object in her hands. Her fingers strayed over the familiar cross and corpus.

"Oh, a crucifix!"

"Yes, dear. A crucifix blessed for the hour of death."

"Oh, thanks. You think of everything!" She raised it slowly to her lips.

Ten minutes later.

"Sister?"

"Yes."

"I used to wonder . . . what have I done for these poor people . . . in the past six months? You all are so useful . . . and strong. I help here and there . . . do what I can . . . but nothing like what you can do for them. Now I see, I see . . . I can give myself in a very special way."

Nine-thirty. Her hand, all speckled with hemorrhages, searched softly along the coverlet. Frances leaned forward and pushed the crucifix nearer. The fingers closed around it.

"Just like a baby . . . ," she murmured. "Can't do anything for myself. . . . A baby in God's arms."

Coma engulfed her. In a few minutes her breathing changed. Monsignor Carroll and the Sisters were told to come. Sister Mercy and Frances Register dropped to their knees and began the prayers for a departing soul. Then they said the *Salve Regina*, for all Maryknollers take leave of earth sailing under the flag of Mary, Mother of God.

121

Eleven o'clock. The breathing stopped. Sister Alberta Marie once Alberta Hanley of Detroit, finished her course. She had accomplished much in a short time.

Sister Alberta Marie rests among the crowds of her beloved squalid poor. Her funeral was worthy of a poor religious. They laid her in a soldier's coffin supplied by the United Nations cemetery. The family carpenter made an outside box of plywood. Johnnie Rhee and Francis, the yard man, worked until midnight to dig the grave.

The Sisters used cotton left over from comforters to soften the bare boards, and they lined the coffin with sheeting. They made a pillow to bear that young head which wore the crown of suffering. Thus she came home borne in an Army ambulance to the foot of the stairway.

The crowds were there as they always were. But there was no idle chatter, no hawking of wares, no sudden flare-ups of temper. They were very considerate, waiting quietly.

As eight young Army and Navy men carried the coffin halfway up the hill to the chapel, the way was marked by a double file of Koreans carrying lighted candles. These were the new Christians she had instructed, the families she had given food and clothes to, the people in the compound who knew her well.

All night she lay before the Blessed Sacrament. All night the Sisters, both Korean and American, knelt in turns. All night the slip-slip of Korean shoes with the funny turned-up toes, sounded on the porch, as people came from the outside and dropped their shoes at the entrance of the chapel.

Oh yes, Sister "Young Person" was well prayed for! The new Christians with stubby fingers laboriously read their prayerbooks. The old Christians whose parents and grandparents—yea, and great-great grandparents too—had endured persecution for the Faith, said their rosaries swiftly. They understood the value of martyrdom. "Unless the grain of wheat die, it remains alone." They saw it happen a million times with every rice harvest. How right it was that this strong young Sister should die that she might bring forth fruit a hundredfold!

In the morning Sister Mercy spread a handkerchief over the quiet face, hiding forever from human sight the features of this Bride of Christ. Requiem Mass began.

Afterwards, the eight stalwart young servicemen carried the coffin further up the hill, almost to the top of the mountain. Here Nakamura San when he planned the garden, had placed a mausoleum for himself. Possibly he felt the view itself would bring his friends to pray for him. Far out over the harbor, almost to Japan itself, sixty miles away, the eye roved enchanted. Nakamura San himself must have toiled up the mountain many times to enjoy the view he would not be able to see when he was a permanent resident in that mausoleum.

When World War II sent him back to Japan, poor fellow, he left his mausoleum behind. Sister Alberta Marie's grave was dug just beside it. It was all very simple and forthright. After the coffin was lowered, the prayers said and absolutions given, the men set about replacing the earth they had removed.

Slowly the crowd melted away. The guests from the Embassy drove away; the chaplains also left. Korean priests and Sisters returned to their homes. The nurses, doctors and servicemen were gone. And before the last shovelful was thrown on the new mound, the Sisters were back among the hundreds of tattered refugees who sought help in their distress.

High up there on the sunny mountainside, Sister Alberta Marie's body was alone with Mother Earth from which God had made it. The mound of newly turned sod was high now, but in a short time, that too would be level once more. The fragrance of flowers left there by her Sisters and friends, the odor of incense from the Final Absolution, wafted over the stricken city, over the warships at anchor, over the broad Pacific Ocean to a heart-broken home in Detroit.

10

Worse, and More of It

"Where do they all come from?"

"Rather, where are they all to go?"

"It beats me!" said Dr. Riberosa, head of the United Nations
Civil Assistance Command. "When you first came to Pusan a
year ago, I knew there was great need for work such as yours,
but I never dreamed of this!"

He and Sister Mercy were standing at the entrance. The
crowds milled around them. The crowd in the street below, the
crowd waiting for injections, the group over in the Orthopedic
tent, the line-up waiting for clothes or food, the thousand or
so mothers with their babies squatting around the Children's
Clinic.

"You didn't?" Sister Mercy laughed. "Why, we used to call
you Riberosa the Prophet. Every week you would come with
something to help us and every week you would predict what
would happen. Something like, 'Next week you'll have four
hundred a day' or 'When I come next there will be shops set
up selling food to these people.' Then you said, 'You'll need a
permanent waiting room' and 'They'll start soon sleeping in
the street here so as to be cared for in the morning.' You're a
good prophet, Doctor. Everything you said has come true."

"Hmmmm," murmured Dr. Riberosa. "How many did you
treat yesterday?"

124

"Just over 2,250, Doctor. Poor people, they had to wait so long!"

"I'm not surprised. Estimates place the population of Pusan now at 1,650,000. That's almost as big as Los Angeles or Detroit. And twice the size of San Francisco, Boston, or Washington."

Sister Mercy added, 'It's almost twice as big as St. Louis and nearly three times the population of my own home town, Milwaukee."

"That's a lot of people, Sister." Dr. Riberosa was serious. "Especially when nine-tenths of them are underfed, sick and in rags. Definitely conditions are not getting any better."

"I'm sure of it, Doctor," said Sister Mercy thoughtfully. "We find that a lot of the new refugees—those who have just come into the city—have very calloused fingers. They tell us that they have been digging for roots to eat along the way. That's new. They used to be able to find something above ground; now they must dig.

"Yesterday, Sister André was called by an American M.P. The bodies of two Korean men had been found on the docks. The M.P. wanted to know if we could do something about having them removed. He was unable to get action on the case and thought Sister's gentle voice might prevail where the Army had failed. About a week ago she had been able to have another body taken away from the street near us. Well, after repeated phone calls to various offices, Sister got the National Police to promise that the bodies would be attended to. But it all adds up to one thing, Doctor. It is much more common now than it was a year ago that people should die on the street without any spiritual or medical aid. That's the thought that drives us on."

Dr. Riberosa faced her. "Sister, take a warning from old Riberosa the Prophet. Don't push yourselves beyond the limit. You Sisters must take care of your own health."

"We do, Doctor, we do. I see to it that everyone gets proper rest and good food. We do not work more than fourteen hours

—only twelve as a rule. But these cases are so pitiful one can't refuse them. Today, for instance, an old man stumbled wearily into the Clinic leading his young grandson who is going blind. They had walked twenty days to get here! The poor old fellow was so worn out from the trip that we had to give him emergency treatment before we could even turn our attention to the boy. When cases like that come to us, we have to treat them no matter how tired we may be."

"What's going to happen to the boy?"

"Dr. Mundy—you know, the eye specialist from the 22nd Evacuation Hospital—will do an operation. He thinks he can save one eye, but the other is hopeless. The old man considers it well worth a heart attack to get such help for the lad!"

"Sister, let me say this. You have certainly gotten relief down to a smooth working system and yet kept the heart in it. That's a real accomplishment."

"How could we do it, Doctor, without the many kind people who help? We have seven doctors working full time, four Koreans, a Swedish doctor, and two American Sisters. Each of us examines about one hundred patients each day. Two other doctors come for regular orthopedic and eye clinics each week. Eight nurses give injections and treatments all day. And the Army nurses continue to help in their free time. That means at least fifteen people, full time, are either examining new patients or treating those who come back for injections, dressings or renewals of their medicine. Besides this medical staff, we have a goodly number of technicians, aides and maintenance help. In all, sixty-two employees are here, besides the eight of us from Maryknoll.

"But we *are* fussy about records. Sister Dolorosa and her staff keep the cards up to date on each patient. She often catches somebody trying to sneak in on someone else's ticket. It's uncanny how she can remember faces! Small wonder they call her Sister M.P.!"

Dr. Riberosa laughed. "Small wonder they call this 'the longest charity line in the world'! Your Clinic here with its pre-fab huts and packing-box orthopedic table tends more children under ten years than any clinic in the United States. I was just looking at the figures in the A.M.A. *Journal* recently. The Children's Hospital in Washington, D. C., has figures which come closest —95,000 children as out patients in a year."

Sister Mercy smiled. Figures are interesting but the whole person is so much more than a digit in medical reports. Medicine reaches one part of him; food and clothes, another. These are basic to the physical life. Beyond that, the whole person needs love and kindness. He requires self-sufficiency, companionship, family life.

She saw her guest to the gate and turned back to the Clinic wondering what could be done to help The Whole Man.

Wednesday was Clean-Up and Stock-Up Day each week. With thousands surging through the place, one had to call a halt once a week to fumigate the place. The floors were scrubbed, the lights and windows cleaned, the benches scrubbed within an inch of their lives with special attention to the nooks and crevices where bedbugs and lice might hide. Examining table covers and cubicle curtains were boiled, ironed and hung up ready for the next week. Ceilings got a brush down and the walls and windows a washing.

The shelves were stacked high with clean bandages and dressings. Shiny ampules of injections stood row on row ready for use. Stacks of tongue depressors and little wooden sticks, new rolls of cotton, big spools of adhesive tape, bottles of alcohol and witch hazel were replenished. Out in the Pharmacy, Sister Rose of Lima and her crew made up literally thousands of doses of vermifuge and castor oil, vitamin pills and chloromycetin.

However, all this did not mean that the "Please Do Not Disturb" sign was put on the front gate. Clinic scheduled for Mornings Only often lasted until 2:30 or 3:00. Any emergency was cared for and those who needed daily attention were told to come on Wednesdays even if the gates were closed.

Wednesday afternoon was the special orthopedic clinic. These cases, nearly all children, came once a week, carried on the back of their long-suffering mothers. Tuberculous necks, spines, hips, legs were encased in plaster of Paris. The poor little tots could not move more than a finger. Fleas and lice, inevitable when people are forced to be dirty, burrowed under the casts and had a Roman holiday on tender flesh. More than one victim dug his fingers through the cast, making little holes all over it. The cast cases were under long-term sentences, one year, two years, maybe more—until the tuberculous bones were healed and able to bear weight. Yet two or three times a week, the women carried their children long distances to the Clinic. This meant bearing the weight of a forty- or fifty-pound child together with a ten-pound cast. And these Korean mothers did not have ham and eggs for breakfast, either.

In May, 1952, more than one hundred children were in casts. By the end of the year the figure had risen to 350.

This is the story of one week in May:

MONDAY, MAY 5. *A beautiful six-week-old baby girl was brought in this morning. The father told us his wife had died on the road a few days ago. He and the entire family of seven children were working their way down from Seoul, accepting whatever work, food or shelter they could get. The baby was born on the road-side; a few weeks later, the mother died of starvation.*

At first he asked us to find a home for the baby. But when he understood that we would provide sufficient milk and clothing for the child, he refused to give her up. "I'm a shoemaker," he said. "I'll keep her on the floor next to me while I work." The poor little thing was crying with hunger, so Sister Magdalena prepared a bottle of milk right away so that she could be fed before she went home.

The burn cases are becoming very frequent lately. Today a boy, ten years old, was brought in with a two-day-old burn. His

arms, cheek and neck were a sight—thickly matted with sea-
weed and other Korean medicines. All this had to be removed
before we could begin to care for the burn.

The new Children's Clinic, a two-story building, is almost
ready now. For several months, Sister André has had a merry
time with her head in a whirl consulting the contractor and
engineers. By now she has a liberal education in electrical engineering. She even knows what she is talking about when she
speaks of voltage, size and type of wiring, what size bulb pulls
how much voltage, and where the sterilizers and autoclave should
go to use our wattage to greater advantage.

Sister André is boning up on plumbing right now, for the
water system will soon be installed. She wants to know all about
elbows, eight-inch pipes, two-inch pipes, and twenty-inch plank-
ing before she has to supervise the job.

TUESDAY, MAY 6.   A little girl created quite a stir this afternoon
when she was rushed ahead of the line into the Children's Clinic.
She had swallowed a half-cup of kerosene. Sister Mercy and
Sister Augusta worked a long time over her. She was much better,
although weak when the treatment was ended.

Last fall a hopelessly emaciated baby was baptized Jude. The
mother brought him in several times after that, then we did not
see him. Today, a strange woman brought a baby who had been
left on her doorstep. She asked us to find a home for him, or at
least to give her milk for this little unwanted one. As the woman
talked, Sister Augusta felt more and more that she recognized
that baby. A search was made through the files. Sure enough, it
was little Jude—and not much bigger than he was last fall. Jude's
Guardian Angel must surely be keeping a sharp eye on his charge.

All in all, our need for milk and baby bottles increases every
day. (They are Coca-Cola bottles fitted with nipples!) Besides
Jude, three new babies were put on milk, all only a few weeks old
but very scrawny. Two of them live in the defunct railroad
station, turned over to the government as a shelter for hundreds
of refugees. The poor mothers were delighted to see us dress the

129

babies in soft flannel garments and caps and stockings. Like all women with new clothes for their babies, they love to take the little ones back into their arms, readjust a pink satin bow or touch up a pretty blue silk bonnet.

We had to tell the third woman that her baby was dying. She wept bitterly even though it is not her own. It had been left on her doorstep and this good woman gladly took it in.

The last baby was "Never-Say-Die Joey," as we call him. Joey came last December when he was just four months old. He still looks like a one-month baby. Never have we seen such tenacity to life as Joey has shown. In the past five months, he has gained and lost, gained and lost. But sheer grit has brought Joey over the hump and we have every hope now that he will live.

WEDNESDAY, MAY 7. The Orthopedic tent was very crowded again today. Dr. Serato, ever-faithful volunteer from the 22nd Evacuation Hospital, and his two corpsmen arrived early. But it was plain he and Sister Agnus Therese would not be able to handle all the cases. Help arrived at just the right time in the shape of two doctors, three nurses and a corpsman from the hospital ship Haven. This staff took care of forty patients, some recasted and some put into their first cast. Improvement in some cases encourages us all—doctors, mothers, children, and Sisters. Their mothers carry the children here on their backs, heavy casts and all. The anxiety of these poor women, their love for their sick children and the length they will go in self-sacrifice, make us more eager than ever to do all we can to help them. Certainly they do their share.

One of those emergencies which make our clean-up days more interesting! An old man of seventy years was carried in on the back of "a young fellow," as he called himself—a man of sixty-eight. Two years ago, the old man had been beaten by Communists and his leg was broken. There is little we can do now, but we will try to get him crutches so that he can get around by himself.

Sister Dolorosa was straightening out her record cards when

a very poor family came in, the picture of dejection. The mother died a few days ago; the father is very sick. He sat panting in one corner of the waiting room while Sister got the information on the case. The two children huddled up close, scared, tired, hungry and miserable.

A bath and new clothing all around were the first steps in rehabilitation. Then arrangements were made to care for the father and older boy. The little girl, just three, can stay here for a while with Patty, one of the women who works for us. To top off a red-letter day for this family, just as Papa and the boy were preparing to leave with food, clothes, and the promise of future help, in came Patrisya with steaming bowls of rice and vegetables all cooked for them. She had seen the family coming through the gate. "They could use a little neighborliness," she said to herself, and set about this task of Christian charity.

Besides all this, a large allotment of clothing came from the Civil Assistance Command. When these things come on Wednesdays, we can get them sorted and ready to give out on the next day.

THURSDAY, MAY 8. More clothing! Huge crates of it from the men aboard the aircraft carrier Bataan. Sister Herman Joseph hired Our Gang to get it sorted and on the shelves of her Bargain Basement. We need it. Each week, an average of 450 people receive clothing here. In addition, forty-five families get rice, vegetables and milk once a week. Usually every day we have five or more emergency requisitions from the doctors for food to be given to people in starving condition. You can see why our shelves never stay full!

The little "kerosene baby" of last Tuesday came back to the Clinic, much improved, thanks be to God.

A very sick baby with a serious liver disease was brought in. The entire little body was a deep yellow color tinged with green. Sister Mercy gave it special attention but feels that it will not get better.

A steady customer at the adult clinic is "The Phantom of the Opera." He is a young man who was severely burned in an oil explosion. By the time his treatment is finished, his entire head, face, arms and chest are swathed in white bandages. We have to cut holes for his eyes, nose and mouth. He would look like a Halloween ghost anyway, but he gets the most drama from his appearance. Hence the title "Phantom of the Opera." He struts down the street with his arms crossed over his chest looking like Lazarus as he came forth from the tomb in winding sheets. Sister Rose of Lima was tempted to put a board on him advertising the Maryknoll Sisters' Clinic, but we all stopped her. We don't need any advertisement!

FRIDAY, MAY 9.   One of our most crowded days, and such desperately sick people that it would take a book to tell about them all.

First, a woman so far gone with tuberculosis that she is nothing but skin and bone. Her feet are badly swollen and yet she had walked a long distance to get here.

Then a two-year-old boy who is only the size of a four-month baby. He was brought from a village seventy miles away. A case of extreme malnutrition and rickets, he has never been able even to sit up. This is the worst we have seen yet.

Immediately after this, a girl of ten was placed on Sister Agnus Therese's examining table. Every bit of her body is swollen up like a tight balloon. She couldn't even open her eyelids the least bit—also due to beriberi and malnutrition.

After her, a very appealing child with the thinnest, saddest face, huge black eyes, who was too weak even to stand.

Leprosy! A little boy Sister Mercy examined proved to have it. Sister thinks the mother probably has it too.

SATURDAY, MAY 10.   Starvation over long periods is taking a terrific toll from our people. Within the last few days two adults have died right in our waiting room. They had nothing with them and no place to go. Nobody who cared, either. They simply dragged themselves all alone to our waiting room breathing their last. Sister Rose of Lima remained with them and tried to make them as comfortable as possible. She recited short ejaculations and prayers while they died peacefully. Then she bathed them and changed their clothing while the crowds watched with breathless amazement. After several phone calls and attempts to reach the city authorities, the bodies were taken away and buried.

Today was a day of unusual gifts, to say the least. In the morning, a grateful ex-patient presented us with twenty baby chicks. She is able now to earn money and has set up quite a little business for herself.

Then, at noon a serviceman brought a thirty-pound snow goose, beautiful with white feathers, huge wings and black feet. The neck is two feet long. The feathers alone should make several pillows and the wings, if we could preserve them, would be perfect for angel's wings in next Christmas's pageant. But Ok Ja, our cook, is not too happy about the goose. She took one look at him and then at her small stove. "How can I ever get such a bird into my oven?" she wanted to know.

SUNDAY, MAY 11. This afternoon, Sister Mercy, Sister Rose of Lima, and Sister Agnus Therese spent some hours working on statistics for the Civil Assistance Command. Taking only the patients who came yesterday—2,219—they listed them according to diagnosis and particular disease. Tuberculosis was the highest—401 cases for yesterday alone.

Morning and afternoon Sunday school classes make our compound nearly as crowded on Sundays as it is on other days. There are 380 persons under instruction for Baptism at present.

"The girls" were lunching at the University Club in New York. They were all career women, mostly in advertising work of various types—copywriters, media directors, public relations, publicity, ad managers. In a fiercely competitive field, they were "tops."

Some were women of deep faith, Jewish, Protestant, or Catholic; others had no faith at all in any organized religion.

Lillian Shapiro, a Jewess, was among them. Her short curly black hair bobbed first to one old friend and then to another. The headwaiter ushered them to their usual table. He knew them—good customers, successful businesswomen of New York.

The talk was general, and genial for the most part. Alice's new job, Joan's successful advertising campaign, Margot's promotion, Madge's latest gimmick to get publicity for her company. But through it all, there were some complaints at life in general.

"My maid didn't show up this morning. Well, really, if this is going to keep up. . . ."

"And I said to my husband, 'Jim, if you can't get me a new car, I'll go out and earn the money myself.' It just isn't fair. . . ."

"After all that, I couldn't get the tickets for the show I wanted to see! . . ."

"I don't think it's reasonable to expect me to walk that far. Of course, I took a taxi."

These and other grievances filled the lunch hour between morsels of tasty food in the air-conditioned confines of the pleasant room.

Lillian's soft voice bubbled into laughter often. Her keen eyes took in the well-cut clothes and the nail polish. These were hard working girls; they deserved everything they had. But suddenly she remembered—

"Listen everybody," she announced, "I want to read you something."

She fished into her dainty purse and pulled out a clipping.

"Oh, *The New York Times*," someone said.

"Yes, it's the 'Letters to the Editor' column for this morning," Lillian replied. A letter from William C. Bullitt—you remember, our former ambassador to Russia and to France. Now listen." And she read:

To the Editor of the New York Times:

I have just returned from Korea. Before the communist attack, Pusan was a poor town of less than 300,000. Today it is submerged by more than 1,000,000 refugees. There is no new housing. The refugees build shacks of old boxes, tin cans and paper. The wind chills their huddled, undernourished bodies. Disease, led by tuberculosis, runs through the swarming streets.

Into these streets Maryknoll Sisters from New York moved in the spring of 1951. All were trained physicians or nurses. At the top of a teeming alley, they set up a little clinic. There, by working eighteen to twenty hours a day, they treat each day an average of the unbelievable number of 1,810 ill children.

The children do not complain or whimper or beg. They are led or carried by their mothers to that one door of hope, and stand or lie on the ground for hours awaiting their turn for treatment. They face their suffering with the same courage that makes the Korean soldiers, when they are wounded, refuse to turn back to a dressing station and crawl on toward the enemy until they are unconscious or dead.

The light that shines from those Maryknoll Sisters and guides their patient hands is not of this world. Each day they give all they have to give of strength and skill and love. Often they come to the end of their earthly resources; but they are the help of the helpless, and always, when there is nothing, Someone provides.

Pain borne as those children bear it rises to pure tragedy. Care given as those Sisters give it rises to saintly love. No work of service that I have ever seen in any country has seemed to me so surely blessed by God. Anyone who wants to help that work to continue should send a contribution, however small, to the Maryknoll Sisters, Maryknoll, New York.

William C. Bullitt

She put the clipping back into her purse. No one said a word. Suddenly their complaints seemed trivial, inconsequential, so vastly unimportant. Lillian looked around them.

135

"Shall we do something about it?" she asked. And then laughed. "This will cost you each a donation!" She put out her hand cajoling each one to make her donation large.

The girls took it all in good part. Who could refuse Lillian anyway? Cheerfully, they reached into their purses and handed over to her what they could spare. Later in the day, she sent the money together with her own generous check to Sister Mercy.

Thus began Lillian Shapiro's work for Korea. From then on, she was tireless. She stretched a chain of compassion from her advertising office in New York to the suffering in Pusan.

"People like me get so immersed in making a living," she said, "that we don't take time to make life worth while for ourselves and for others."

There was the touch of advertising genius behind it all. Lillian's first campaign was a chain letter: I write ten letters to you and you write ten letters to people you know. There was no beating around the bush with Lillian. She said right out, "Come on, send some money to those Sisters in the Clinic."

The fertile brain soon concocted another scheme. Operation Lollipop! Candy companies were the victims—or did they come out on top? Lillian made the rounds of the companies asking for donations. But she also put her friends on the spot to go out and buy lollipops. Poor things! They did it laughing, too. Thousands of old-fashioned suckers crossed the seas to Korea for children who had never seen the like before.

Operation Lollipop was a lot of fun—hard work, too, of course—but then Miss Shapiro got down to sterner things. To fight malnutrition, she launched—Operation Vitamin.

This took salesmanship. She went from one drug company to another. She walked out of many an office with a carton of expensive vitamins under her arm. "And the executive often escorted me out to the elevator as well," she exults. "Maybe he wanted to make sure I would go!"

By this time, Lillian Shapiro was head-over-heels in the work. She brought everything to bear on it. Her deep faith in her own religion, her keen mind and bubbling sense of humor combined to wheedle the most out of many who would otherwise be perfectly content to be innocent bystanders in the fight to save lives.

She said once, "Every night, I ask myself, 'Have I done something for Korea today?' And if I can't find anything in the day's work, I hop out of bed and make a phone call, or write a letter, to ask somebody for help."

Her Operations became well known. *The New York Journal American,* and *The World-Telegram* gave her generous space. The Catholic magazines carried on the publicity. Of course, the news-peg everywhere was, "Jew Helps Catholic Nuns." It never turned that curly black head. Miss Shapiro, advertising executive, knew that publicity can help any campaign.

Her friends poked good-natured fun. "Taking the veil, my dear?" The climax came when a letter was received at Maryknoll addressed to "Reverend Mother Shapiro."

"We're still laughing, the Sisters and I," Lillian said. "I told Mother Mary Columba that her job is safe."

The last operation—Operation Adoption—was born of an incident at the Clinic.

Sister Agnus Therese was treating a three-year-old child. The condition was serious; the little girl needed treatment every day. But Kap Sugie, the mother, came only twice a week. Like most doctors, Sister Agnus Therese could see only the patient's side of it.

"You must bring her every day," she told Kap Sugie several times. "Otherwise, I cannot hope to cure her."

Kap Sugie burst into tears. "I can't" she sobbed. "I have four other children at home. My husband went to war and I think he is dead. Unless I work, how can I get food for us all? And if I come here every day with this little one, how can I work? Ai Go! Ai Go! The child will die, but I cannot let the others starve."

Sister Agnus Therese wrote of this as an example of how badly

137

needed was a hospital where the children could be left and cared for while their mothers earned a living for the rest of the family. Kap Sugie's was no isolated case.

Lillian Shapiro heard about it. Operation Adoption was planned to provide the necessities for Kap Sugie's family for a year.

"Every friend to whom I told this story offered to help," she said. "These friends told other friends. And so it goes."

Operation Adoption pushed through to a successful conclusion. Kap Sugie's family was cared for for a year. Across the wide Pacific, the war widow of Korea sent her thanks to the advertising woman of New York:

"I would like to thank you hundreds and thousands of times. I have five in my family and we were starving and my baby sick unto death. We could not pay special attention to her and she was expected to die, but you and your friends helped her and she is as strong as any other child now. And you helped all my family from starvation and nakedness. You are the kindest people in all the world. We shall thank you through our whole life."

"Working late?"

Sister Augusta stood accusingly before her Superior. As the Assistant, she felt she should keep a watchful eye on Sister Mercy. So often the light burned far into the night in that tiny office with the waxed paper windows and the baked clay *undol* floor.

"So many people to be thanked! When they work so hard to collect medicines or to send us money, I just can't brush them off with a stereotyped thank-you." But Sister Mercy put down her pen.

"I know! So you write them a nice letter and they're so thrilled about it they send more help and then you write them an even better letter—and so it goes. The packages come from all over."

"They can't come too big or too many for me!" Sister Mercy laughed. "We need all the help we can get from any source whatever. NCWC Catholic Relief Services just sent $1,500 for rice. It's a lot, but with rice at $60 a bushel, how far will it go? And drought has ruined the barley crop this year. . . ."

Sister Augusta leaned forward. "Listen, Sister. I guess you and I have been thinking along the same lines. For the past four months we have been averaging between 2,000 and 2,300 patients a day. That seems to be the point at which we will level off. Things are getting worse, as you know, but it is not due to more refugees crowding into the city. Rather, the refugees here are dying off from long-term starvation. They need the medical care we give them, of course, but if we could do something to solve the basic problem. . . ." Her voice trailed off.

"I was thinking that, too," Sister Mercy agreed. "These people need other things. Housing, and jobs, and security for the future. In our early days here everyone thought the war would be over and the people would go back to their farms. But truce talks at Panmunjam have dragged on for over a year. The refugees stay around Pusan. Nobody's going to go back home and begin life over again when a stroke of a pen might put his farm in Communist territory tomorrow.

"In the meantime people have to eat. Babies are born, old folks are dying, boys and girls should be getting ready for school. Life goes on. We have to face it. Things are bad and they are going to get worse."

She was silent. Sister Augusta waited a moment.

"Go on. Go on," she urged. "What are we going to do about it, Sister? I'm sure you have something in mind."

"We can't do much, but the little we can do, that we ought to attempt, at least. I have a few projects in mind.

"First for the war widows. Some 300,000 Korean soldiers have been killed or wounded—that's twice the figure from all other United Nations forces combined. I would like to get decent houses built for them. Oh, I know we can't do anything on a large scale, but by September we may have fifteen built and I hope thirty more before the winter sets in.

"Then many women need work. And they do such beautiful sewing! If we had a workshop started, we could give them work to do. If it were properly managed, I'm sure we could dispose of their products.

"Another idea is this: Remember Ok Soonie, the terrible burn case? That little tot will be scarred for life just because her mother had to leave her alone while she went out working. If there were some sort of a day nursery to care for children, we could lift a terrible burden of worry from many mothers.

"I'm always thinking, too, of the thousands who are too far away from the Clinic to come in. Besides, Sister Agnus Therese cannot carry enough in her bag to treat many patients. If we had a truck outfitted as a mobile clinic which could make regular trips to outlying districts. . . ."

"Dream on, fair dreamer, dream on!" Sister Augusta teased.

"All right, my dear, I will," Sister Mercy rose to the bait. "Here's something else. It's a scheme which the people at NCWC broached. They call it Adopt-A-Family Plan. People give $5.00 a month to help keep a family in food. The materials are bought here—rice, turnips, yams and things Koreans are used to. Of course, $5.00 won't buy enough food for a month, even in destitute Korea, but it will be a good basis for a family's rations.

"Donors in the States would be greatly encouraged if we could get back to them a personal letter of thanks from the family they helped. The National Council of Catholic Women might take up the idea. Remember how they got seven tons of candy from Schrafft's for us last Christmas?

"And always, glimmering up there on the horizon of my dreams is a hospital. Mmmmmmmm! Pusan never did have enough medical facilities to care even for the pre-war population. Think of a place where we could give proper care to these children. No lice to carry typhus; no fleas under the children's casts; enough water to keep clean with; and the poor mothers would not have to carry their children to us day after day for months. Oh, Sister, can't you see it . . . ?"

"Come down to earth. You're up in the sky, Sister Mercy," said the implacable Practical One. "Do you realize what all this would take? We are only eight Sisters. You would need a platoon of Maryknoll Sisters and an army of Korean helpers."

Sister Mercy chuckled. She knew a secret. Opening the desk drawer she took out a letter.

"Read this," she said, and sat back for the reaction.

"Well, what do you know! An Honorary Degree! Marquette University is proud of you,—and so are we! But how does that help the Korean situation?"

Sister Mercy set her lips together.

"When I go to the States in June, with God's help I'll come back with something besides an honorary degree.

11

Background for the Portrait

Luxury! Sheer luxury!

Sister Mercy sat back in the plane seat and just enjoyed it. Thirty hours in which to fly high above a troubled world. No phone calls, no visitors to show around, no disputes among the help to settle. No Sisters reporting, "The shipment has come and I can't find a corner to put it in."

She never minded the tug at her skirt when the hand of poverty pulled it. To tend the sick all day, even the importunate and grasping sick? Oh, that was easy. But being Superior demands so much more. To arrange work so that each Sister will have enough but not too much; to provide the little joys of convent life; to authorize expenditures and check on extravagances; to be available and helpful to any visitor at all, whether it be a private from the Army Fire Company come to show you pictures of the folks back home, or a group of visiting Generals from Japan—these things took a lot out of her when her mind was preoccupied with the suffering poor.

"But why should I measure the time?" she examined her conscience. "These are important for the work, too. Besides"—and this consideration always settled matters for Sister Mercy—"religious obedience has laid both tasks upon me. Why love one more than the other? Both are God's work."

She smiled, remembering the day that Johnnie Rhee had appeared at her office door.

142

"Some soldiers outside want to see you," he announced flatly.

"Who are they?" she asked.

"Don't know," said Johnnie and left.

"Probably a couple of homesick lads," she sighed as she put her work away once again.

At the gate, however, she found six generals in full panoply, ranging from General Maxwell Taylor, Commander of the entire 8th Army with three silver stars on his collar, to a couple of one-star generals and including General Pak of the Korean Army.

"I saw stars for sure that afternoon," she thought. "Mostly my lucky star!"

She sank back in the seat again and watched God's white clouds scud over God's blue sky. God all around her—above, below and on both sides. God inside of her; God inside of everybody she saw or thought about. God, God everywhere!

"Just let me steep in You for a while," she thought. "I'm going to think of Your loving care of us, all these past months and thank You step by step for it."

The three of them coming from Japan. The first days of unpacking and setting up the Clinic. Treks up the muddy hillsides. Patients coming to the Clinic. More patients. Still more. Work for the Sisters. More and more work, yet always done cheerfully. God bless their good spirits!

Sister Herman Joseph's clothes and food lines. Sister André working on blueprints for new buildings. Sister Alberta Marie in the pharmacy, her young face lighting up, so eager to help in any way. Sister Alberta Marie teaching doctrine to a group of women. Sister Alberta Marie in chapel leaning toward the tabernacle as to one she loved very much. Sister Alberta Marie laughing as she stood in the doorway showing off her speckled arms. The pretty face lying there on her pillow that Sunday when they thought she would pull through. Sister Alberta Marie saying, "It will be strange and different now to come back after I thought I was going to die."

143

Looking out the plane window, Sister Mercy remembered her own answer. "I had an experience once like that."

She still felt the squeeze on her hand and the words, "And see what God has let you do for Him since!"

Sister Mercy spoke directly to the Almighty. "God, You have been so good to me!"

The plane, the sky, her own grey Maryknoll habit dropped away. She was Betty Hirschboeck again. Betty Hirschboeck, a pre-med student at Marquette University in Milwaukee. Young, lively, with many friends. Among them, Anne Gonner of Dubuque was perhaps the closest. Anne's father was editor of a Catholic paper and was just then in Milwaukee on business. Her brother Nick was a freshman at Marquette.

"Papa's going to take us home to Dubuque, Betty," Anne said one day. "Why don't you come and spend Thanksgiving at our house? John Schroeder and Fred Stem will be there, too."

It was a perfect holiday. Crisp snowy weather, good food, young hearts. Grandma Ritter was there, grandmother of the motherless Gonner children: Clarissa, twelve, Henry, six, and Aloysius, who preferred to be known as "Uzzy," four.

On Saturday morning, the old-fashioned touring car stood ready to take them back to Milwaukee.

"Better pull down the side curtains," called Grandma Ritter, waving from the front porch. "It's going to snow. Goodbye!"

Gaily they rode along. Someone struck up a song:

"Though it's time for parting
And my tears are starting
Leave me with a smile."

The country road wound in and out in those pre-super-highway days. The touring car went at a fair clip up hill, down dale, over gullies and creeks. They were on a bridge some twenty feet above an ice-rimmed creek when it happened. A sudden skid on hidden ice. A wild careening. The car spun round, turned on its side, slid off the bridge and fell—miles it seemed—into five feet of water.

Betty never knew just what she did. Crouched inside the car, she climbed out the door which was now above her head. Fred and Nicky had been thrown out. Standing in the icy water up to their waists, they tried to locate the other three in the wreckage. John and Anne were dead when they found them. Mr. Gonner, his foot pinned beneath the car, was semi-conscious. Betty held his head above water and prayed with him. But he stopped breathing before help came.

Several men came from the nearby farmhouses. They hustled the three survivors out of the water and up to the nearest house. In no time, the farmer's wife had decked Betty out in some of her own clothes topped off with her little girl's sweater. They were kindly people.

"Come and eat," they urged, sitting them down to a huge dinner of pork chops, potatoes and sauerkraut. But they could not eat.

The boys were badly shaken. Betty talked to them like a little old grandmother. "We can't let ourselves go to pieces. We have to keep up for Mrs. Ritter's sake."

It was Betty's task to call Mrs. Ritter and break the news. She called her own parents in Milwaukee, too. Connections on the old, hand-rung phone on the kitchen wall were not so good. She decided to go back to Dubuque to be with Mrs. Ritter, and that evening she went to the Dubuque railroad station to meet her mother who had rushed on from Milwaukee. Of all who had survived, she alone was no worse for the experience.

No worse? Much better. It intensified something that had been growing ever since high-school days—a sense of dedication to a life spent for the poor, the lonely, the ignorant; in short, "those who sit in darkness and in the shadow of death."

Ever since high-school days, Betty had wanted to be a missioner. She used to pore over the books and magazines.

"If they can do it, so can I," she said. The first step was to

145

write to Mother Mary Joseph at Maryknoll and tell her about it. Several letters went back and forth. Mother Mary Joseph in those days of 1918 led a valiant but scanty corps of mission-minded women, as yet unrecognized as a religious community and as yet unable to send missioners to the field. But Mother Mary Joseph could see farther than today and tomorrow. She moved surely and with daring.

"Since you are delayed in coming here to Maryknoll," wrote Mother Mary Joseph, "why don't you begin to study medicine? Doctors are needed on the missions and we have no M.D.'s among the Sisters here." Betty blinked and gasped. She had thought of nurse's training, but medical school?

However, she plunged right in. She took it as an order from one whom she already regarded as her religious superior. It meant eight long years of study before she could enter Mary-knoll. She set herself to a long task. Her studies were expensive, of course, and Betty tried to earn what she could to keep herself in pin money.

Sister Mercy marvelled at the wisdom of Mother Mary Joseph. Clearly, God chooses His instruments with care, like a surgeon selecting the exact grade of suture he wants for a specific job. At that (Sister smiled at the thought), a good Superior is rather like a suture. She binds the parts together, going through them and over and under them. She must have resiliency as well as strength; otherwise, she'll tear through both parts and leave them wounded. In the end, she disappears, losing herself in the growing flesh, and yet leaving her mark upon the healthy tissue. And always, she must remember that she is only catgut in the hands of God. Mother Mary Joseph was like that—and more. With clear vision and a strong hand, she steered her small community straight through to an ideal. She wanted religious women —obedient, docile, quick to respond to direction. But they were not to be stereotyped. Each should flower in the special talents that God gave her. The result would be beauty in variety.

"It is easy enough," Mother once wrote, "to produce Sisters

146

all turned out from the same mold. We have attempted something more difficult."

"How right she is!" Sister Mercy said to herself. After twenty-four years in religious life, she felt that Mother Mary Joseph was years ahead of her time.

The special marvel to this Sister-doctor was that Mother should have told her, a mere name at the end of a letter, to go on to study medicine and then to enter Maryknoll. How did she know it would turn out all right? That Betty Hirshboeck would justify her confidence? The answer is, of course, that Mother Mary Joseph did not know it. She followed an inspiration of the Holy Spirit. Prudence fortified with daring; daring tempered with prudence. Compounded together, they make a good Superior.

Betty Hirshboeck arrived at Maryknoll in 1928 with her medical license in one hand and her baggage checks in the other. She soon felt at home with the other hundred young Sisters-in-training called novices. Their white veils and irrepressible giggles lightened the hardships of pioneer life. They were shown an old apple orchard across the road and were told, "The Motherhouse will be built here someday." For the seeds of growth were visible even then. Betty Hirshboeck was entering a small religious order of fewer than three hundred women. At Maryknoll, they slept here, there, and everywhere on the property—in houses, carriage sheds, a barn, and even the top floor of the business offices. They ate in a converted barn and prayed in a small stone chapel built in the center. They walked from one building to another in snow, rain, or sunshine—and loved every minute of it. And yet, less than six years after recognition by Rome, the Maryknoll Sisters had spread out to China, Korea, Hawaii, and the Philippines, for Mother Mary Joseph lost no time in doing what she had set out to do—send American Sisters to foreign missions.

Twenty-four years had changed so much, and yet the spirit was the same. In 1952 Sister Mercy, M.D., was one of more than 1,100 Maryknoll Sisters. The big Motherhouse was bursting at the seams; a wing must be added soon. Hundreds of Maryknoll Sisters were on missions—in Africa, Central and South America, as well as in Asian countries. They worked not only in hospitals and dispensaries, but also in schools, social service centers, religious-teaching teams—almost any kind of work one could imagine. "All we need now," one had said, "is a good lawyer and an undertaker."

Sister Mercy smiled. So many newspapers said that all Maryknoll Sisters were doctors or nurses. Far from it! She was one of twelve doctors, and all together there were only 114 nurses. But there was a goodly contingent of students in both fields as well as in medical technology, pharmacy and other allied professions.

What had twenty-four years done for Mother Mary Joseph? She who had given this great mission movement for women its first push was giving it now her final gift—years of paralyzed suffering. She was stricken in March of 1952, but her mind was still keen, her decisions still hewed to the line. Although Mother Mary Columba had taken over the work of Mother General, the congregation still benefited by the Foundress's long experience and prudence. Oh, there were few women in this world who could out-think Mother Mary Joseph! She always was on her guard against those who would canonize her before she was even dead.

A newspaper reporter, Sister Mercy remembered, once asked Mother Mary Joseph for a statement condemning a certain South American government just then in power after a ruthless suppression of the opposition party. There were Maryknoll Sisters in the country who had suffered from the new pro-Communist government.

"Some of the opposition party who fled to the States would like you to make this statement to arouse public opinion," the reporter explained. "Then pressure can be brought to bear on the present government so that the opposition members will be released from vile concentration camps."

"I see!" said Mother Mary Joseph. "They want me to get their friends out of jail and put my own Sisters into it."

The newsmen laughed. He knew he was well parried. "Mother," he said with a bow, "for someone reputed to be so holy, you are also very smart."

"You will find that I am smarter than I am holy, young man," Mother laughed back at him.

That was Mother's kind of holiness—very simple and direct, no involvements or tortuous systems of spirituality. The spirit of the law—the basic reason for which it was formulated should prevail over observance of the letter. And charity was infinitely better than meticulous observance of the rule. On this, she brought up her thousand and more daughters.

Yes, Maryknoll had grown so in the twenty-four years since Betty Hirschboeck, M.D., had presented herself as the veriest beginner in religious life! But the same spirit which spread itself over that heterogeneous collection of houses and barns and chapels that was the Maryknoll of 1928, still prevailed, spread now over the world. Thanks be to God for it! What was it that Sister Alberta Marie had said as she squeezed Sister Mercy's hand?

"And see what God has let you do for Him since!"

"Has let you do for Him." Not, "what you have accomplished for Him." That was the crux of it, wasn't it? "God has given to us the privilege of caring for His poor," Sister Mercy wrote once. "It is nothing that we do for Him. It is, rather, another of His gifts to us."

You cannot understand Sister Mercy, nor the work she and her medical team wrought among the refugees of Pusan, unless you have some idea of life in a religious order. This is the soil in which they grow. It is the tie which binds them together and gives them their greatest effectiveness.

As Sister Mercy's plane sped across the Pacific in June, 1952, other Maryknoll Sisters in ships, planes and trains were converging on the big Motherhouse at Maryknoll. They came from large schools in Hong Kong, Manila and Honolulu; from one-room thatched schools in Africa or the Caroline Islands. They came from the six-hundred-bed hospital in Kandy, Ceylon, and the twenty-four-bed Riberalta Hospital in Bolivia. They were teachers, doctors, nurses, social workers, domestic workers. Some had Ph.D.'s; some had only the common sense that God and a high-school education gave them. As far as languages went, collectively they could speak Chinese, Japanese, Luo dialect and Kiswahika from Tanganyika, Spanish, Palauan, Singhalese, Tagalog from the Philippines and Quechua Indian from the Andes.

Some of these Sisters had endured three years in Japanese concentration camps during World War II; others had served in Communist prisons in China; still others were veterans of California roads in the hinterlands where, choking with dust, they searched out the lost lambs of St. Peter.

In other words, I am trying to tell you that these Sisters, although they wore the same dress, were as varied a group as you could hope to find in any assortment of fifty or so women.

And why were they coming to Maryknoll in June, 1952?

They came to attend the General Chapter, a general assembly of delegates from every section of a world-wide mission field. As the duly elected representatives of the Maryknoll Sisters in their own regions, they formed the extraordinary governing body of the whole congregation. Their chief duty in the weeks of Chapter meetings was to elect a Mother General and a General Council of four, who would govern the order for a term of six years. Supreme authority is vested in the Mother General, but there are decisions in which the consent of the General Council is required.

This democratic process of gevornment has been going on in religious orders for centuries. Our own Presidential elections are based on it. Every Maryknoll Sister has some share in determining who is to govern the congregation.

Once elected, the Mother General appoints the lesser Superiors. This is like the president of a company placing department heads. However, unlike Sisters, the office worker has no voice in deciding who is to be president of his company.

The General Chapter also formulates policies on questions of general interest. Any Sister, anywhere in the world, may suggest a topic to be considered by the General Chapter.

Such is the work of the Chapter. The by-products are equally good. Old friends who haven't seen each other for ten or twenty years, meet and laugh over the gladsome days of the novitiate. Years in the jungle or on an atoll of the Pacific are rolled away, and they are postulants again, Mary Baker from Brooklyn and Susie Jones from Wisconsin, fresh and foolish in religious life.

Sisters in charge of operations in different parts of the world compare notes. For instance, Sister Mercy was eager to see Sister Imelda from Hong Kong who had sparked a housing development for Chinese refugees. They were both in refugee work, Sister Mercy providing medical care, Sister Imelda relieving the housing and school scarcity. Sister Imelda was planning to send a Sister-doctor to Formosa; Sister Mercy's experience would be helpful. This give-and-take of community life is of great value to any project work.

Nevertheless, a Sister is primarily a religious and only secondarily a professional worker. Obedience with her should not only be prompt but also joyous and peaceful, with perfect faith that God will supply for her own and the Superior's deficiencies.

It is this very dedication of her entire self—mind, body and soul—to be used exactly as God directs through lawful authority, which makes her ministration so effective. God must love paradoxes. He delights to bring success out of failure, beauty out of ugliness, strength from weakness, life from death. The meek are thrust aside and trampled on, then, first thing you know, there they are inheriting the earth! And still being very meek about it. This must annoy the aggressive to tears.

With His own special brand of foolishness, God confounds the wise. It's a potent mixture. Don't drink it, unless you want to be wiser than Solomon and more beautiful that the lilies of the field.

To place difficulties in the hands of God and let Him work them out in His own way and at His own speed—this it is that eliminates frustration and leaves you ready to seize the first opportunity for improving things.

One of Sister Agnus Therese's letters from Korea puts the paradox aptly:

> *I am a little fearful to realize the place we have in people's estimation. It is a serious responsibility to represent the God of love!*
>
> *Yesterday morning early a dying baby was brought to my examining room. One glance sufficed to tell me that it was truly dying. Both mother and father were there and I asked Sister to say a few words about God and Heaven while I examined the little one.*
>
> *They were not poor people; rather, they had a good education and knew something of what Christians believe. They readily consented to the baptism and I did it immediately, pouring a few drops of water on his head while saying, "I baptize thee Joseph in the name of the Father and of the Son and of the Holy Spirit." In a few minutes the heart stopped; there were just a few little gasps and he was gone.*
>
> *I turned to the parents. It must have rent their hearts to see their chubby nine-month-old baby die. But I found them consoled already. I stood there with my stethoscope on the baby's heart and my hand on his head while they explained.*
>
> *"We knew our little Yong Min was dying," the father*

said, *"because yesterday our regular doctor told us that he could not live. Both lungs had an overwhelming pneumonia. After he left we talked it over and decided that if Yong Min lived through the night, we would take him to the Clinic so that you might put your hand upon him.*

"We live quite a distance from Pusan. At three o'clock this morning we hired a car and brought our baby to you. We are content now that we have done all we could for him. He lived long enough for you to put your hand upon him."

It is not the first time this sort of thing has happened. These people came, not for Baptism, for they have never heard of Baptism. Nor because they had faith in our medical skill, for they were resigned to the baby's death. God, Who is pleased to reflect His love and mercy in our unworthy selves, drew them on without their really knowing why.

Enjoying this privilege of being a sort of mirror for God —albeit a dusty and smudgy mirror all too often—how can one be anything but always happy in His service?

Sister Mercy came back to Pusan in August with her eyes shining and her pockets bulging—with promises, anyway.

An ovation for her had rocked the big Milwaukee Civic Auditorium as she stood to receive the hood of a Doctor of Science, conferred *honoris causa* by Marquette University. The blue and gold of the hood brightened her Maryknoll grey while 12,000 people applauded uproariously. She was—for the moment at least—Marquette's pride and Milwaukee's darling. The last to subside were the brand new M.D.'s, just finished with eight gruelling years of study and now released to a lifetime of gruelling service to others.

In New York, she saw officials of Catholic Relief Services which had sent already hundreds of thousands of dollars in medicines, clothing and food. Plans for the Adopt-a-Family program were completed. Two hundred families were to get steady supplies every week.

Other relief agencies also heard her story. American Relief for Korea agreed to allocate clothing and medicines.

Hoffmann-LaRoche, where a new drug for tuberculosis was being perfected, talked over with her the results of the drug as used in Pusan. She was told the Clinic had the largest concentration of TB of the bone among children they knew of. Reports on this drug as used there would be enlightening, to say the least.

Best of all, six new Sisters were slated for Korea. Two were old Korea-hands, Sisters Gabriella and Eugenia. They could start right in with new projects. The other four were young Sisters. After a stint of language study, they would relieve pressures in the pharmacy, laboratory and receiving office. Already Sister Anne Charles was nominated Assistant M.P.

12

An Inheritance of Holy Cards

Tai Sook had a pretty good idea of what was happening to him. He had seen others go this way. At times when he roused to consciousness, realized his filthiness, and looked at the underside of the cigarette carton which was his roof, he thought he must be dying. At least he hoped he was. If he weren't so terribly weak, he might help the process along to a successful conclusion. But by the time he mustered his mind to devise ways and means, he had lapsed into half-coma again.

Those were the nice times. He could forget himself—the dirt, the stench, the bed-sore, the ulcer on his leg, the nipping, teasing vermin, the dribble of blood from his last hemorrhage which had hardened on his chin and cheeks.

He was Comrade Min Tai Sook then, Young-Man-On-the-Way-Up in the Communist Party. Party Organizer Kang spoke highly of his indoctrination classes. "You have the real ideology, Comrade Min," he said. "They will be taking you to Moscow for party leadership courses some day."

"Labor!" Tai Sook had thundered to the class of young boys in training as Communists. "Labor makes everything. Labor should get everything. Down with land-owners! Look! Who makes your cloth? Who saws your wood? Who grows your rice? Labor! Labor produces everything!"

"But Comrade," a scared, little voice had piped up once, "many times it happens that a man labors well but without rain and sun he produces no rice. Labor cannot give sun or rain."

"Can you tell me, O wise one," Tai Sook had withered him, "what does produce the sun and rain?"

"Well, I had thought that something—or someone—we do not know exactly—something outside of our natural knowing—some person too big for us to know," the young student had stammered.

"And what or who is too big for us to know? Modern science has found the answer to your question. Very simple, . . ." and he told them about heat rays from the sun so many billions of miles away, and explained how light years measured the distance of the stars, and showed how rain was made when vapor condensed due to cold air on the mountain tops. The vapor? That was lifted from the earth's water expanses by the sun's heat. A touch of conscious simplification poured out in his tone, for he wanted this young sprout to realize just how ignorant he was. It befitted him more to listen than to ask questions.

The boy was stunned by the vastness and complexity of simple things like rain and sunshine. He said nothing when Comrade Min finished, but the question was big in his eyes. "My goodness! And did man's labor produce all that?"

Comrade Min was too bright himself to be convinced by his own explanation. But it sounded well and dazzled the ignorant and seemed an effective answer to the old boogie which lurked behind these impertinent questions. That is, the humble—and humiliating—acknowledgement that man is dependent on some supernatural being or beings.

"He is NOT!" Comrade Min would say to himself, as if vehemence would compensate for soggy reasons. "Man is free! Man is strong! Man makes his own destiny! Workers of the world, unite! Too long have we been serfs of the land-owners! Too long slaves of the factory! We have kow-towed to the priests too long! Hate them all! Hate Japan! Hate America! Hate God!"

And when you run out of things to hate, just keep on hating.

Conscious again. His eyes opened and Tai Sook saw the cigarette carton lettering above him. "Rich Americans! They and their cigarettes and their chocolate bars and their well-fed children!"

Then he remembered his fellow-comrades. They were well off, too. Up North some had made a pretty pile for themselves. Quite a few had sneaked over the border and were living well. Comrade Kang was right here in Pusan.

Where were they now when he needed help? Young-Man-On-The-Way-Up was now Young-Man-Down-And-Out. He curled his lip at the bitter truth. He had always known that was the policy: "Use them and throw them away." Only he never thought he himself would be discarded.

He tried to change positions; the bed sore pulled away from the burlap sack he lay on. He bent his knee and the ulcer scraped along the rough sacking. The little actions stirred the lice and fleas to new activity. He wondered dully what day of the week it was. No food for so long! Three days, maybe.

Oh, the salty taste in his mouth again. He knew what that presaged—another hemorrhage. "Make it the last! Please, please, make it the end for me," he begged of nobody in particular. The blood rose from his lungs and trickled out the corners of his loose hung mouth. Once more he blacked out.

Something soft and wet, sweet and cleansing passed over Tai Sook's mouth and chin. A hand gently lifted his leg and flexed the knee to a more comfortable position. He felt himself turned over. The filthy rags were cut from around that sore on his back. For some time he just let himself be handled, not wishing even to open his eyes lest the spell break. Then he was rolled back, softly, softly, and he knew he was resting on something sweet and clean.

With a sigh he opened his eyes and stared into the faces of two queer creatures. One was a Korean face, smooth and untroubled as a child's and yet strangely mature. She wore a black veil with stiff white stuff framing her face. She worked steadily and fast, wringing out her cloth in a basin beside her, rubbing soap on it and applying the warm cleanness of it to his chest.

157

The other was an American face framed in a veil, too, but one that came to a peak over the forehead. She was the one who had lifted his leg. She was cleaning the ulcer there now.

His sigh had startled them. The Korean smiled. "Now that you are conscious," she smiled, "better take some of this." She poured hot soup from a thermos bottle. Together, they held him up while he sipped it slowly. He asked between sips,

"What are you going to do?"

The American answered. "We'll get you comfortable before we leave. Tomorrow, we will come back and take you to Young Do Island where you will be cared for in a little sanatorium we have there."

"Why do you do this?"

"Because God loves you and we love God."

"Silly!" he said with what little strength he could muster. "Ignorant! Talk like that keeps our people subservient. You can tell God for me that I hate him!"

The Korean Sister said in a matter-of-fact tone. "That doesn't keep Him from loving you."

He wanted to scream, "I don't want Him to love me!" The effort was too much. He lapsed again into unconsciousness.

For the first few days at Young Do, Min Tai Sook lay content to be clean and fed. He hardly knew how he got there. In a jeep, he sort of remembered, to the foot of the hill. And then by jiggy-frame carried by a porter for the rest of the way up the mountain. There was a Sister along—one of those American ones—must have been Sister Rose of Lima for she came out every few days to check on the patients and to bring new ones. She was the moving spirit behind Young Do. But for the present he did not care who nor how; it was utter happiness to know that he was there, that he was clean and that he would get food.

"Thank you. Thank you so much," he said often to Agada, the Faithful One, who took charge of the little sanatorium.

Neither he nor they referred to his last message to God.

Young Do was for just such men as Min Tai Sook. Destitute men dying of T.B. Sister Mercy had built it before she went to the States, using packing boxes for the floors and flattened tin cans as shingles for the roof. Painted white, it nestled in the green trees on top of the mountain. Small, but clean, airy and restful, it served well as a springboard for Heaven.

Tai Sook rallied. He began to take an interest in his neighbors. Beside him was Kun Nam, a young fellow still in the early twenties. He was really in a bad way—probably would not last more than a week, breathing fast and short, constant fever, eyes too bright for health.

Between hemorrhages, Kun Nam lay very still on his pillow looking often at quite a collection of religious pictures arranged as he liked them on a board at the foot of his bed. At night, when the pain was worst, he gasped, "Jesus!" or "Oh God, take me, take me!"

Tai Sook kept his own counsel. Since he was well treated by God's servants, he refrained from insulting their Master. It was only good manners.

Agada and Kun Nam had quite a joke together about his dying. You might think that Heaven was right next door. Agada had many messages she wanted Kun Nam to give her friends there. "You won't forget will you?" she used to say. "Tell Our Blessed Lady that I'll be along just as soon as she wants me. But I want to bring a lot of others with me so they won't notice old Agada slipping past the gate."

"I'll be there, Agada," Kun Nam would answer. "You keep praying that my purgatory will be short so that I can give you a real reception."

Kun Nam noticed Tai Sook's eye straying over to the holy pictures more than once. "Take one," he invited. "Any one you want."

"I can't," said Tai Sook.

"Why not? I have plenty. I'd like to. . . ."

"I don't mean that," said Tai Sook. "I don't know God. For years I've told students He doesn't exist. How can I come crawling to His feet now? I won't; that's all, I won't!"

Kun Nam burst out laughing. That set him coughing. And

159

that brought on a hemorrhage. It was early evening before he was quiet and rested again. Tai Sook leaned out of his bed and whispered through the dusk. "Why did you laugh at me, Kun Nam?"

"I was thinking," came between gasps. "I was thinking . . . that you are like . . . a man dying of thirst . . . beside a beautiful clean lake. . . . You refuse to drink from it just because . . . just because (he almost laughed again) . . . you didn't know before that it existed."

"Oh," said Tai Sook slowly.

"Remember, Comrade Min," Kun Nam went on. "Remember this. You have to get on your knees to drink from that lake."

"I'll never do that," Tai Sook was positive.

"Odd!" commented Kun Nam. "I said that myself once."

Kun Nam died a few days later. Tai Sook inherited his holy cards.

When her labor pains began in the early evening, Suk Myunie was just where she didn't want to be, that is, on the other end of town from the Maryknoll Sisters' Clinic.

Well, there was no help for it. She had come out there to beg because there were so many more Americans around that section. But pickings were slim. She had to push herself to whine and pluck the sleeve of the passerby; and who bothered with one more silent figure of misery hunched against the brick wall? Besides, now that Chung Doh was getting puffy from malnutrition, he got very little sympathy. What was it the two Wacs had said? Oh yes! "Do look at that darling little fat boy! They can't all be so poor as we hear."

So Suk Myunie raised herself up from the street and took Chung Doh's hand.

"Where are we going, Omani?" the four year old asked.

"Omani is sick," she told him. "Come along. We have a long walk tonight."

Together they walked through the crowded streets. Suk

Myunie sometimes went down in a lump of pain. The child waited docilely beside her until she stood up again. She went down for longer intervals and rested oftener, as the lights went off one by one and the streets cleared of traffic. Several times she crawled between buildings to rest, and found the crevice already occupied for the night.

By midnight, she knew she wouldn't make it although there was only a mile or so to go now. She lay still beside the concrete abutment of a bridge and waited for the birth of her baby. Chung Doh, poor boy, had been stumbling from weariness anyway. He could roll himself up in the barley sack, as he did every night, and fall asleep.

Suk Myunie had no very clear idea of what she would do with the baby when it was born. She really hadn't thought that far ahead. Her goal had been to get to the Clinic, a goal she had set many months before when she took Chung Doh there for an infected ear.

"When my time comes," she had said to herself, "I'll come here." But that had been in the balmy days when she had been working. Her husband was in the Army and got down to Pusan occasionally. They had a shack then with even a floor in it. Then he came no more and she heard he was captured by Communists.

As the months advanced and she could not work, she had sold the shack and everything for food.

It was maybe three o'clock when she started off again, this time with the new-born one in her arms. Chung Doh kept close to her. It was painful, but she made the rest of the way in slow stages. In an hour or so, she sat herself down just outside a back gate of the Clinic to wait for dawn.

The alley was deserted. If she had turned the corner, she would have found a crowd lining up for the morning opening. She preferred to be alone; there was The Problem to think out.

Should I? Or shouldn't I? In her malnourished body she knew there was no milk for the baby. Supposing the Sisters did give her milk powder for him and all the equipment as well. How could she heat it, and keep the bottle clean, living as she did on the street, moving from one good begging spot to another? How could she come all the way back here for further supplies of milk powder every three or four days? Chung Doh was failing—was it right to keep another hungry child?

On the other hand, suppose she left the little one right here beside the gate. The Sisters would care for him and find a home for him. Every week the foster mother would bring him for a check-up. He'd develop into a roly-poly, a beautiful, strong, intelligent baby with red cheeks and shoe-button eyes. And eventually a handsome active boy—who would never know his mother.

"I can't!" Suk Myunie whispered fiercely hugging the bundle to her. "You're mine. I can't leave you here. And yet. . . ."

And off she went again on the same round of reasoning.

At six Johnnie Rhee found her. He always checked the back gate for abandoned babies in the morning. She started up guiltily, as if to run away. But she had dallied too long. The Problem was already settled.

Sister Agnus Therese came down to examine her. She found her in fair condition; she had taken pretty good care of herself. Two men came with a stretcher. Suk Myunie was only too grateful to lie on it and let herself be carried up to "The Plaster Tent." Chung Doh held her hand all the way up.

Sister busied herself getting things ready. Over in a corner stood bags of plaster of Paris. In the center of the tent was a table-effect made of two packing cases. Boxes of gauze bandage were stacked beside a crude sink. Several old casts stood in a corner, like an eerie collection of bodies.

"You'll be all right here for a few days," Sister said, clearing away some small pieces of equipment. "We won't need this tent until Wednesday. By that time you'll be able to go to Blessed Mother Mountain."

It meant nothing to Suk Myunie. All she cared about was a clean dry place to sleep in and the prospect of food she could share with her baby.

Four days later she was as good as new. So was Chung Doh. His swelling had gone down so fast Sister Magdalena said it was like pricking a balloon. It was always amazing to the Sisters, to see how quickly these starvation cases responded to vitamins and food. Suk Myunie showed herself anxious to help in any way she could. Chung Doh already acted like a charter member of Our Gang. They looked like good prospects for Blessed Mother Mountain, a tent colony of war widows set up to care for just such cases.

Suk Myunie was washing out bottles for the pharmacy one morning when she saw the Well-Baby Clinic in operation. These hundred or so babies had all been abandoned at the clinic. Either they were left at the gate, or thrust into someone's arms while the mother said, "Hold him until I come back," or quietly left behind in a waiting room to be discovered when everyone had gone.

At first Sister Mercy took them to an orphanage run by the St. Paul de Chartres Sisters. But the Sisters could not accommodate so many. Several were taken in by women living on the property, but that refuge, too, was soon exhausted. Then one morning a beautiful girl was left at the gate. Sister Augusta washed and fed her and decked her out in the prettiest baby clothes that famous bargain basement of Sister Herman Joseph's could produce. She put her in a cardboard carton near the stove in the waiting room. Above her was a sign:

DOES ANYBODY WANT ME?

Before the morning was out several had applied. Even when this particular baby had been carried home triumphantly, others turned in their names, saying, "I'll take the next one."

The arrangements were simple. The new parents were to register the adoption in the City Hall. The Clinic would provide milk, a Coca-Cola bottle and a nipple. Every week on Wednesday morning, the baby was to be brought for a check-up. At the same time, the adoptive mother was given the week's supply of milk. Seven hundred and fifty pounds of whole dried milk was used per week.

163

Suk Myunie watched the babies with tear-blurred eyes. Then she picked up her infant and covered his tiny face with kisses.

Sister Herman Joseph writes home:

September 16, 1952

I spent this afternoon at Blessed Mother Mountain, the little colony of war widows we are housing in tents on the north end of town. You would have laughed to see The Black Beetle (that's what everyone here calls our jeep—painted black with Maryknoll Sisters blazoned on the sides) as we started out from the Clinic. I was bringing out wood and cardboard which the women use to reinforce the canvas tent walls. Also a sewing machine and materials for quilts. Not to mention a woman and her small boy and new-born baby—who was born in the street a few days ago. And me, to boot. The Black Beetle can really carry loads.

It was wonderful to see the welcome extended to Suk Myunie. To say the truth, these twenty-one families living in four tents are crowded, so I hated to bring another family. But the women all laughed and said, "Oh, we can always make room!"

They took the baby from Suk Myunie's arms and showed him to all their children. "He's going to stay with us, so be nice to him!" She gave him to one of the little girls to carry up to the top of the hill. The jeep cannot get us to the top: much of the stuff always has to be transported by hand. They carried up all of Suk Myunie's bundles, too. These contained the food and clothes we had outfitted her with. "Don't worry about supper," one of them told her. "We'll find something for you."

The sewing machine has a story attached. About five months ago we listened to a sad tale of woe (there are so many!) from a young woman who was sure she could earn a living if we gave her money to start a little sewing buisness.

The end of it was that we did, although sometimes it seems like a foolish thing to do. Not a word from her from that day until just yesterday when she appeared at our front door saying she had succeeded in the business venture. "I have two sewing machines now," she said, "and I want to give one to you to thank you for getting me started."

It was truly a God-send. For some time we have wanted to expand our quilt-making. Winter is coming on and, to a destitute Korean family, a quilt can serve as bed, chair, rug and everything else combined. Mama, Papa and the whole family roll up in it at night. We were counting up the other day and I believe we have given out at least 5,000 quilts in the last year and a half. This winter, if we have them, we could give out several thousand more.

The project is also a means of livelihood for our war widows at Blessed Mother Mountain. Already they are working on reconverting American clothes into something Koreans can use. (We get the wildest styles in the clothing bundles— ball-gowns and ballet slippers and Hallowe'en costumes.)

The tents are big things, 30 x 24 feet, provided for our war widows by the Civil Assistance Command. As we approached them, I was surprised to see six Korean soldiers digging foundations for a new tent we hope to put up soon. We have been wanting to get this done for the women but so far we had not been able to get labor for it.

Han Ah Junie explained. "A few days ago in that big rainstorm, one of the tents split wide open and the whole framework tipped to one side. The next day, some of us were trying to get it fixed when these soldiers came over from the barracks over there. We told them about this project and they pitched right in to help. They have been here every day since."

Just then the Korean Commanding officer came along. I held my breath lest he order them back to the barracks. Instead he asked all about it. When Han Ah Junie finished, he said,

"It's a good thing. Most of us soldiers don't know where our wives and families are, either. We'll help." He turned to me. "Su Nyo, tomorrow I'll send a hundred men to put up this new tent and make the wooden platform for the inside." Was I relieved!

The last thing that happened was very nice, too. Just as I was getting into the jeep to return home some of the children came tearing down the hillside. They had missed the excitement for they were up in the woods picking flowers all afternoon. They loaded me down with a bouquet which would choke an ox. But as I bounced away in the jeep I couldn't help but think that two months ago these same children were sloshing around in the filth of Pusan's streets. Thank God they have flowers to pick now and a good clean mountain to pick them on!

Someone careless had sparked it in the dead of night. Suddenly the whole hillside was ablaze. Like a flood washing down straws, flames rolled over huts of driftwood, cardboard and burlap. And before the roaring breakers of flame ran the refugees.

Elizabeth Reid was in the middle of it all. Her camera and notebook worked overtime. She ran ahead to climb a wall for an angle shot; she picked up bundles to help some poor woman along and got her story as they both ran for shelter. She carried injured children. She comforted lost ones. And she took pictures, pictures, pictures.

Best place for pictures, she thought, would be the Maryknoll Clinic. Monsignor George Carroll, in charge of NCWC relief supplies, would be there giving out clothes, blankets and food. The Sisters would no doubt be tending the injured. The fire was only a half-block away from it.

She was not wrong. The Clinic was a blaze of lights. Half-dazed crowds milled around the gates, looking fearfully over their shoulders at the black smoke which poured from the red fields behind them. Firemen were knocking down blazing walls and telephone poles on one side of the wide main street. On the other side, crews of men formed hand to hand bucket brigades to pour water on the smoking houses lest the fire leap across the street.

Half a block away, Johnnie Rhee, Francis Han and Bernard Sin were wetting down roofs of the Clinic. Their half-naked bodies glistened with sweat although it was January. Sparks flew through the air and more than once Johnnie danced when he found a roof too hot to stand on.

Elizabeth pushed her way through the crowds and came into the compound. Clumps of people here and there were family groups waiting to collect each other. Others were lined up awaiting medical attention. Inside the Clinic, doctors and nurses were working as usual, while the water poured off the roofs and the air was close with smoke and soot.

There were surprisingly few burn cases. By November, 1953, a Pusan refugee always slept with one ear open for the crackle of flames. But there were many cases of cuts and bruises, people trampled underfoot, half suffocated with smoke. The paths through the refugee sections were narrow and slippery. Rushing madly to get out of danger, people were knocked down and kicked, or they fell and broke their bones someplace. In the dark, some had stepped on broken glass. Others were carried in by relatives, utterly exhausted. The worst was a fractured spine.

It was not physical ills which troubled most of them. Rather, the hopeless prospect of beginning all over again. For months they had carefully built up the most tenuous kind of security— a shack, a quilt, a *kim chi* jar and a rice pot. Now the shack was burned to the ground, the rice pot was broken when Papa fell, the quilt was snatched from Mama's arms by a thief operating in the frantic crowd, and the *kim chi* jar had to be left behind because it was too heavy to carry. Small wonder they sat on the ground and let stupor take over.

Monsignor Carroll was a bulwark of cheer to cling to. He spent the night giving out quilts, clothes and what he had of household goods. He ran a Lost Children's Bureau which also took on Lost Husbands, Lost Wives and even Lost Grandmas.

American Army officials were all around the place. Some stood ready to move out valuable equipment should the Clinic catch fire. Others guarded key points lest a looting mob smash through the gate. Looting was rampant in the black market stands on both sides of the flaming main street. General Whitcomb, Korea Base Commander, himself came twice to check on the Clinic's safety. His own car and that of Ambassador Briggs stood at the back gate ready to evacuate the Sisters.

However, by three in the morning, the ocean pumps were functioning and a long hose had been connected to carry the water all through town to the area. With a steady stream pouring on the blaze, it was yielding to treatment. What had been a field of flame was now smoking black. The main body of the fire had worked its way behind the hillside where the Clinic was.

The lines of patients had been cared for. There only remained the job of helping families to find one another, to comfort the dejected, to give out supplies. Sister Agnus Therese and Sister Paul Francis (one of the new Sisters, a pharmacist) started out to see what the fire looked like. Elizabeth Reid went along with them.

They climbed in the sooty darkness up to the further limit of the Clinic property. It was high, but not high enough. Bernard's home up there was really a back gate, for the rear wall of his house was part of the fence. The three adventurers passed through the house and out of the compound. They were on a leveled-off space, once a school playground but now, like the rest of the mountainside, covered with matsheds, huts and shacks of thousands of refugees.

They were all out to watch the fire, a huge area, an inferno of blazing frameworks. They watched it as an African lad might watch a lion gnawing at its kill. Will it see him and pounce? Or is it too busy with one kill to bother with another? Each family had brought out their poor valuables so as to be able to run at

168

the first change of wind. Many had little stands—the family's entire business venture—where apples, or thread, or pencils could be sold on the sidewalk. They were easy to pick up and move whenever prospects seemed brighter someplace else, or if the police came around asking for licenses or getting too inquisitive as to where they got the stuff.

Suddenly a terrific explosion sounded on the far edge of the flaming area, a great mushroom-shaped puff of smoke rose.

"An atom bomb?" asked Sister Agnus Therese, incredulous.

"Oh no," said Elizabeth. "Some gasoline drums stored over there, that's all. That heavy black smoke is from oil deposits. You might say a prayer or two that the ammunition dumps don't go up."

It was plain that the firemen were coming out on top in the battle. Cutting wide swathes through the mess of flimsy shacks on all sides of the blaze, they had fenced it in.

"It will burn itself out in the center there, now. Let's go back," said Elizabeth. They turned and came down the hill. Not wanting to disturb Bernard's household again, they decided to skirt the outside of the Clinic property and enter by the front gate.

Thus began the education of Elizabeth Reid, veteran newspaper woman. In her day she had covered fires and murders, wars and bloodshed. She had specialized in refugee stories from Hong Kong, where thousands were fleeing Red China daily to jam into Hong Kong. But this was something new.

To begin with, it was pitch black except for the flashlights she and the Sisters carried, and some few kerosene lamps held by family groups as they huddled tight around their quilts and rice pots. Thieves were millions that night, like mosquitoes on a summer evening.

The narrow paths were slippery, half-frozen and worn smooth by the tread of countless feet. Worse than that, they were jammed with people. Half the hillside wanted to get down to the level street. On the other hand, thousands of people from the burned area were pushing up the paths looking for some tiny cleared space where they could rest until morning. Squirming, wriggling, shoving, grunting, yelling, each man was for himself and Devil take the hindmost. Any who slipped and fell could be trampled to death.

Pickpockets made hay in the darkness. They grabbed the refugee's quilts, thrust their hands into pockets, cut the clothes off one's back. Elizabeth clutched her camera with both hands and used her elbows alone for clearing a way. More than once she felt a hard tug at the leather strap around her neck. A Sister beside her guarded the gadget bag. People behind thrust her forward; people in front pushed her back. It was a nightmare.

Sister Paul Francis called out to a woman struggling up the hill, a patient at the Clinic.

"Did you save anything, Kum Nae?"

"Oh no, *Su Nyo*, only our lives," she answered with difficulty. "I got the baby on my back and took Yon Ah by the hand. We ran. . . ." The rest of the answer trailed off as she was swept past.

At the bottom of the hill things were better. Trucks had come at General Whitcomb's order to take the homeless—estimated at 8,000—to large warehouses, which had been turned over as temporary barracks for them.

Elizabeth and the two Sisters were able to slip into the clinic compound.

Preparations for breakfast were underway, not for the Clinic personnel, but for the family groups which dotted the whole compound. Luckily, Monsignor Carroll had purchased rice just the day before. This would be cooked and packed into balls, (where were there rice bowls for so many?) and distributed to the adults. The Korean Sisters were already making gruel for the children. Sister Herman Joseph came up with some cookies that had been donated as spoils from a blackmarket raid. There would be enough for all, thanks be to God. Thanks be to Him also that the Clinic was safe. A change in the wind would have wiped it out.

170

One by one, the Sisters dropped into chapel for a Thank-You visit and went off to rest for an hour or so. It was around 4:30 A.M.

Sister Mercy stayed up. That is often the way with Superiors. They send everybody else off to bed and take the hard work themselves. Elizabeth wandered over to where the mobile clinic was parked. It was another gift from Catholic Relief Services. Sister was inside checking on supplies. Were there enough bandages for the burn cases? How about splints for broken bones? Merthiolate for the cuts?

"Those people who were jamming up the hill tonight will be back at their old places tomorrow," Sister explained. "We can send the mobile clinic down there for a few days and bring it back here at night to restock it. Let's see! We ought to have a number of food and clothing tickets here, too, so that needy cases can come here and get what they need."

The crowds were there as usual at regular Clinic time. The early days when they formed one long line were over. Now, with more personnel, more tents and pre-fab buildings, the crowds could be split for quicker handling. Besides, many were old customers at the Clinic. They knew the system and delighted in telling new-comers just what to do.

Elizabeth watched Grandpa Han at his self-appointed duties. Having "made Han Gap," that is, passed his sixty-first birthday, he was honorably retired. Nobody expected him to contribute to the family income. He was free to exercise his real talent—Unofficial Host to the Clinic's thousands.

"What an emcee he would make!" thought Elizabeth approvingly, seeing him at work down in the street.

"This is your first visit? And the baby is sick? Right here to the Examining Line. And you, you're sick yourself? Well, the Adult Clinic is over there in that place at the top of the steps."

"You've been here before? Good! Take the baby to the injection line right there."

"That looks like a very sick boy you have! If you show him to Sister over there, I think she will let him in without waiting."

"Ai Go! Ai Go! You belong in the food line. See that small place? It's the laboratory. Just around the corner from that is where the food is given out."

Two lines formed in front of the Adult Clinic each morning. One was for newcomers to be examined and diagnosed. The clinical laboratory on the grounds was most important here. In a situation where the patient could not be hospitalized, specimens had to be analyzed quickly if a scientific diagnosis was to be reached. No medication was given until an accurate diagnosis could be made. It would be fatal, for instance, to confuse tuberculous meningitis with infectious meningitis. In the other line, old patients came for injections or treatment already prescribed.

Many lines of women with children formed before the four Pediatric Clinics. To the General Pediatric clinic came all the acutely ill. More than fifty percent of the children had tuberculosis, but results had been splendid through use of the new drugs.

At the Immunization Clinic, vaccines against tuberculosis, smallpox and whooping cough were used. Every child who came to the Clinic was vaccinated against the last two, and, if he showed a negative tuberculin test, he got the first as well. As soon as a case of smallpox was found in the Clinic, a nurse accompanied the patient to his home. There she rounded up all the children in the area and vaccinated them immediately. The program of vaccinations was carried into the homes, the schools, the refugee camps and orphanages.

"Peanut-butter kiddies," as Sister Mercy called them, lined up at the Malnutrition Clinic. Practically every child in Korea was malnourished; many were on the verge of starvation. Besides the food supplies given his mother, each child received a paper container of peanut butter and a tongue-blade for a spoon. And away he went on Mama's back, perfectly happy with his world.

The fourth Clinic for children was Orthopedic. Here came

the real old friends of the Sisters. In each of the four hundred cases of TB of the bone, mostly of the spine, the child received at least two years of medicine and food as well as the gradual correction of the deformity. After many months in a plaster of Paris cast, the small patient graduated to braces. UNKRA supplied funds for the development of the brace shop. The Orthopedic Clinic took money and time and infinite patience. But oh, it was worth all that when Sin Tok, or Dong Hwan or Song Young stood up straight and really walked with his hands at his sides. And the Sisters would look at his mother and they would remember him as a tiny frail little tot, bent over double and hobbling along with his hands on his knees. Oh yes, it was worth it a thousand times over to the mother who carried him like a great white mummy so far and so often to the Clinic.

Best of all was when he came back to show Sister his school uniform and books! This *was* rehabilitation, as the Welfare Workers termed it.

With the soot still on her face and the smoke of last night's fire clinging to her clothes, Elizabeth took a turn around the compound on the hunt for good pictures. She came across Nazareth Workshop quite by accident, ducking around behind the main Clinic building. This was Sister Gabriella's domain. She was teaching a group of women the intricacies of embroidery and painting on towels, napkins, place mats, table cloths and all sorts of linen and silk novelties. Using their own quaint design, the women produced nice souvenirs for servicemen to send home. Some thirty families were supported through this project, working in their own homes.

Elizabeth Reid decided to drop into chapel before she went home. She went up close to the tabernacle and prayed.

"Dear God, look at the things these Sisters have been able to do with just a Clinic in make-shift buildings. You know what they need, don't you? Please, why don't You give them a hospital?"

13

An End and a New Beginning

Twelve months and some 503,000 patients later, the dream began to come true. Fairy Godfather took the form of Brigadier General Richard S. Whitcomb, Commander of the Pusan Military Post.

He really didn't look much like a fairy godfather. For that matter, neither did Myong Sukie look much like Cinderella. Her face and hands, her whole skinny body in fact, were horrible with impetigo. Scabby and malodorous, she played around in Pusan's streets making them even more diseased than they were.

And then—whoost, my dear!—along came Fairy Godfather in his golden coach and scooped her up and took her to where the angels in white are. He hustled her out of the shiny military car with the white star painted on it, and turned her over to the head angel. No, not an etherial being arrayed in flowing clouds, but a very solid angel with a chocolate bar in her hand for good little Myong Sukies. She remembered in a daze that Fairy Godfather said something like, "Sorry. Can't stay. Have a meeting at Headquarters. But do thou take care of her and I on my return will pay thee all."

Then he left. Just like that. Myong Sukie didn't know the Bible or fairy stories very well—in fact, not at all. If she had . . . well, when she returned home all bandaged and clean and smelling of dermycin, she might have boasted to everybody of

riding in Fairy Godfather's golden coach, or even on the Good
Samaritan's donkey. As it was, being a refugee child in Pusan
with three years of grubbing in the gutter behind her, she told
them that the No. 1 American Big Shot in all of Pusan had
driven her in his car to the *Su Nyo* to have her sores treated.
They didn't believe her. No Big-Nosed Foreigner could possibly
love a scabby child in Pusan that much.

At that, there was something unbelievable about General
Whitcomb's care for every human being. He found himself in
charge of thousands of American boys, away from home for the
first time, plunked into an Oriental city of a million and a half.
The truce talks had dragged on for two years; an armistice was
signed. But there was no real end to war. The boys were not a
fighting army; they were men waiting for something to happen,
either one way or the other.

The work of the troops was routine—lots of it, but boring.
With the shooting stopped, it seemed to have less purpose. They
wanted to go home and could not. Yet here were the volunteer
organizations working day and night in an effort to help destitute people. Why not put the two together? Give the boys useful work to do, work that would give them a stake in the
community, and provide the agencies with more help? Not only
could they be a godsend to the welfare workers, but they could
carry out big works that only an army can do.

Myong Suki was a real little girl with a real case of impetigo.
She really rode to the Maryknoll Sisters' Clinic in General
Whitcomb's white-starred car. But in a larger sense she is a
symbol of Pusan. For the General found her ugly and bleeding,
fire-scarred and resentful. He left her started on the road to
recovery.

When I was a toddler, my aunt always liked to clean me up
for the afternoon. "It is so rewarding," she used to say. Fixing
my sister, who had no affinity for mud, wasn't nearly so satisfy-
ing. The sight of Pusan, cleaner and healthier than she had been

in her long history, must have been very "rewarding" to General Whitcomb.

By this time, the emergency caused by the influx of a million refugees in 1950, had congealed to a status quo. In 1954, in spite of the relief given by other agencies—the Benedictine Sisters, the Australian Presbyterians, Baptist missioners, Seventh Day Adventists and others—the crowds at the Maryknoll Sisters' Clinic grew. In one day, an all-time high of 2,597 patients streamed through the examining and treatment rooms. The monthly figures rose from 36,000 to 47,000 in June, just four years after the first shot of the Korean War.

The truth was plain enough; endurance was giving out. A man can be hungry for a week or a month, maybe a year. But when he is hungry for four years, has seen his wife and children die from hunger, has been burned out of his home several times, has shivered through four winters and sees no respite for the fifth—that man is sicker in mind than he is in body.

General Whitcomb was not one to stay behind his shiny desk and read nicely typed reports. He was here, there and everywhere in the city. He had a habit of dropping off at the Clinic any time at all, just to mosey around and see what was doing. If one of the Sisters spotted him, she came forward with a welcome. But much of the time, he came and went without fuss.

The first result of these fact-finding cruises was the Troop Aid Program. Fourteen young service men from Colonel White's 44th Engineers reported to Sister Mercy one morning. "What do you want done, Sister? We're here to do it."

Cement walks between buildings, an incinerator, shelters for waiting patients, fire-proof tin roofs on various buildings, a cement foundation for the water tank, an asphalt driveway and parking lot—these blessings poured from the Troop Aid Program. Eventually the 32nd Quartermasters' Group built an entirely new Orthopedic building. Other volunteer agencies fared as well.

The General went on to wider projects. AFAK, Armed Forces

176

Assistance to Korea, was born. The general plan behind these big projects was: the Army would supply materials and engineering Know-how; the Korean Government would give the land. Little by little, several battalions of ROK Infantry came to Pusan for training in construction work under American engineers. Then they were placed on jobs and a new group went into training.

By early 1954, General Whitcomb was juggling houses, schools, roads, a drainage canal, an artificial lake, orphanages and a tile factory. All these good things required teamwork. The American Army, the United Nations Korean Relief Agency, the Korean Government and Army, the Pusan City authorities got their heads together. Or, if you prefer it, they put their shoulders to the wheel. The results were worth while.

At Tongnae, 111 homes were built; at Young Do, 109. They were for fire victims. Not enough for everyone, of course, but still a help to the situation. A tile and block factory was erected to provide materials to make these homes. A broad highway, known as Maryknoll Road because it ran right in front of the Clinic, was graded, widened and paved. A double purpose was accomplished: the road was a good by-pass around crowded downtown streets and, in case of fire, it enabled fire-fighting apparatus to reach the honey-combed hills.

"Lake Success" was the ironic name of an evil smelling pond that drained half the city. These twenty acres of horrible water had no outlet to the harbor. A canal, thirty feet wide, was dug right through the main road and straight across the port's busiest quay, Quay #2. Spanning it, a mammoth bridge, only thirty feet long, but wide enough for six bridges, carried the railroad, the Port Road and all the restless foot-traffic of an Oriental seaport.

Sixteen schools were either constructed or repaired. The Chosun Christian University was rehabilitated. Pusan National University received a new plant for its School of Engineering, and moved its entire campus to beautiful Tongnae, on the Eastern outskirts of Pusan, where the Engineering School was being built. These school projects ranged from running in a water line or furnishing desks and benches, to rebuilding the entire school from the ground up.

In the fifty-three orphanages in and around Pusan, the children were used to seeing American servicemen come calling with laden arms. Many times, a unit took a whole orphanage of kiddies under its wing. Now AFAK contributed materials to rehabilitate a number of these homes for children, and to move others to more wholesome locations.

In the middle of this intensive program, General Whitcomb hurled a bolt out of the blue to Sister Mercy. He said casually, "How would you like to have a hospital?"

The hospital project was a seven-headed venture. To talk it over, seven Volunteer Agencies met at the Maryknoll Clinic on March twentieth. General Whitcomb outlined the plan as he hoped it would work out.

To begin with, in all of Pusan, there were only forty hospital beds available to the general public. This was the need—dire and urgent—that must be met. To relieve the situation, he proposed building seven hospitals with a total capacity of 570 beds.

The Army would supply construction materials; General Maxwell D. Taylor, commander of the 8th Army had given permission for that. Army engineers would oversee the work. The Korean Government would either give the land outright or sell it at a very reasonable figure. It was up to each agency, however, to pay for the labor on the project and to equip its building for hospital work.

Even with all the help proffered, these two items—labor and equipment—meant a heavy outlay from each agency. To give some help on it, however, the General had another scheme.

He would stage a fund-raising campaign among the soldiers, similar to the Community Chest or March of Dimes drives in the States, asking each one to contribute only one percent of his salary. He left it up to the agencies themselves to recommend how these funds were to be divided. Without hesitation, they accorded Maryknoll Sisters' Clinic the lion's share of 44 percent of the total, since the Sisters had been working in Pusan the longest and handled the greatest number of patients. The Board of Officers that had the final allocation took the agencies' recommendation and made it their own decision.

To help in the campaign, the General arranged for the servicemen to visit the various Clinics. Units from out of town were brought in by bus. Every day, two non-commissioned officers were stationed at each dispensary to show the men around and to answer questions. General Whitcomb wanted the boys to see exactly what their money would go for.

Things moved swiftly. On April thirtieth, the campaign opened. In May, the Korean government sold the land for the Maryknoll Hospital at a low price. Even the governor of the province himself, Governor Lee Sung Yong, made a personal trip with General Whitcomb to Seoul to expedite the government's action on the land. During the hot summer, a mammoth thermometer in Pusan's public square told the campaign's progress. High spot and final round-up of the whole affair was a carnival over Labor Day week-end. In three days more than 43,000 G.I.'s and their guests milled through the carnival grounds trying their luck. The most popular game was "Dunk the M.P." When you hit the bull's eye with a ball, a fully clothed real M.P. fell into a tank of water. Not only was it good for a laugh but the M.P. got a chance to cool off on a blistering Labor Day. He didn't mind too much. General Whitcomb decked out in a complete Korean costume, was one of the sights worth seeing. Altogether, the carnival netted over $70,000.

Meanwhile, the works went on. The Tongnae houses were finished in June; the Young Do project in July. The drainage canal and its bridges were completed in April. By mid-summer, troops camped on made ground in the center of old "Lake Success." Bulldozers, steam rollers, asphalt spreaders and hun-

179

dreds of laborers were grading and paving the Kukje Market Road and Maryknoll Road.

The Seventh Day Adventist Hospital of thirty beds stood practically completed. The Baptist Hospital (seventy beds) was ready for the cornerstone. Plans for a hospital of eighty beds to be staffed by the Australian Presbyterian Mission, and one of one hundred beds known as the Children's Charity Hospital were nearing completion. A T.B. hospital to care for one hundred patients and a small pediatric unit of thirty beds were in the planning stage. The big Maryknoll Hospital with a potential of 160 beds was ready to start. It was July 29, 1954.

General Maxwell D. Taylor, himself, came from his headquarters in Seoul. He thrust a shovel into the soft earth and pressed it down with a business-like foot. He bent over so far as almost to crack his stiff new uniform, then cheerfully he straightened, tossing a healthy shovelful of dirt to one side. On that hot afternoon, the beads of perspiration on his face shone as brightly as the four silver stars on his collar.

Up there on the grandstand with the generals and notables, Sister Mercy hoped she would not disgrace them all by crying. It just didn't seem possible. Three and a half years of work in makeshift buildings with wood stoves in winter and blistering tin roofs in summer. Years when pitchers and basins were standard washing equipment. When operations had to be delayed or foregone completely because no facilities were available. Years of struggle and hard work but oh, of such real joy in working together to the last ounce of strength. It really hurt to see mothers standing hours in line so that their babies might have two or three minutes of a nurse's time. And it was heartbreaking to treat a child, knowing that he must go back to the same little shack, overrun with rats, infested with fleas, which had given him the disease to begin with. Harder still to lie awake at night and listen to the heavy cold rain falling—to know that through the long dark hours sick Koreans were lying on straw mats on the street outside. And yet, without a hospital, it had to be so.

Was it really three and a half years since the three of them had stepped from the plane, the first civilian women permitted back in Korea after the war's outbreak?

Yes, this ground breaking for the long-dreamed-of hospital presaged a new era. With mixed emotions, Sister Mercy heard the earth drop from General Taylor's shovel. She knew it was her Nunc Dimittis in Korea.

She was ready to go. Indeed, she knew she must. Her health was breaking. This last year, she had just dragged herself around. Mother Mary Columba knew it and had appointed a successor, Sister Angelica. Sister Mercy was told to come home. She was to rest and recuperate for a few months. Then a new task was waiting for her, to start the first non-segregated hospital in Kansas City, Missouri.

Negro doctors there were without a first-class hospital to receive their patients. A delegation had approached the late Archbishop O'Hara asking him to provide a Catholic Hospital for Negroes.

"I am not interested in a Negro hospital," he told them. "But I am very much interested in a hospital to care for *all* the sick, negro or white." It was a missionary venture; he asked the Maryknoll Sisters to take it on as such.

The needle goes first and makes the stitch; the thread follows after and holds it. Sister Mercy was a very fine needle.

The last speech had been given; the last song sung; the military band packed up its instruments and went home. Eventually the last guest was seen to the door. Sister Mercy had been properly extolled and farewelled.

Earlier in the day a twenty-bed T.B. sanatorium at Kam Chun, succeeding the little white Young Do refuge, had been dedicated. This, also, as the other, was for destitute T.B. cases dying on the streets.

Tomorrow she would leave for the States. Only a few little things remained to be done. Thank-you notes could be written on the plane tomorrow. But tonight she wanted to say good-bye to the faithful Korean helpers—Doctor Rhee, Nita the nurse, Patrisya and Bernardo, Johnny the gateman—oh, to them all!

Just a few days before, Sister Mercy had spoken on the problem of T.B. of the Bone before the Korean Ministry of Health in Seoul. Officials had taken the opportunity to make her an honorary citizen of the capital city. Then she had gone to visit Agada, now conducting an orphanage on the outskirts of the city.

Tonight, too, she must talk again with Sister Angelica, newly come from Bolivia to take over the Superiorship. They were old working mates. Sister Angelica had succeeded Sister Mercy in Bolivia in 1950. In the 1930's they had been next-door neighbors, so to speak, when Sister Mercy was a doctor in Korea and Sister Angelica a nurse in Manchuria. Now, after two weeks together, Sister Angelica was to carry on.

It was no easy task. Only the foundations of the hospital were completed. General Whitcomb, spark-plug of the whole campaign, would be retired from the Army and leaving in a few weeks. The armed forces were pulling out gradually. Definitely, Sister Angelica could not expect the help that, up to then, servicemen gave individually or in groups. Yet it was her task to complete and equip that big hospital.

She had twenty-two Maryknoll Sisters to work with, three doctors, a corps of nurses, technicians, pharmacists and other professions. The crowds still came each morning; the babies still died; the children still starved; the men and women were diseased, but now not hopeless. A new lift was in the air. Housing projects could care for only a small fraction of the homeless, but at least that fraction had homes. Fires still broke out, but fire engines could get there in shorter time. Schools might be dilapidated, but there were benches to sit on and books to study.

KAVA (Korean Association of Volunteer Agencies) was welding together the work of some fifty-three welfare groups, striving for the rehabilitation of the Korean people. Sister Gabriella served on the committee to aid War Widows. Her Nazareth Workshop was supporting some sixty families in useful work.

The emergency was being stabilized at last. Tremendous work was still to be done, but the facilities to do it with were there.

As she lay in bed that night, bits of the laudatory speeches of the afternoon's function came to Sister Mercy's mind. Letters and citations from the Ministry of Health and the Mayor of Seoul, from the Korean governor, from the Mayor of Pusan, from General Whitcomb and other officers—they were formal and sometimes flowery in Oriental style but a genuine warmth poured through the phrases.

Choe Byung Kyu, Mayor of Pusan, slight of build and hesitant in his English, had said it best. The Clinic, he said, had provided medical treatment, food and clothing, milk for babies, work for war widows and "religious ministrations to those whose souls crave religious understanding."

"Now before your departure," he finished, "you have made possible a large new hospital for our people. All Pusan and the world that comes to this great port will look up and when the lights are turned on in the early evening, they will see this hospital standing on its high hill. They will say their thanks to you, Sister Mary Mercy, M.D., for the great work you have done for suffering persons and the great example you have given of the practical workings of the Faith you represent."

Ah, that was it! Mayor Choe pierced through the incidentals to the core. Sister Mercy's whole life, all her activities in any sphere whatsoever, showed forth the Faith that was in her. The Koreans had sensed that. They saw the Sisters not as welfare workers grappling with a tremendous social problem, fine as such work might be, but as Sisters driven on by the charity of Christ to the utmost in service to man.

The Sisters saw Christ suffering in the Koreans.

The Koreans saw Christ loving them in the Sisters.

In Christ, they met.

To YOU—and You, and You!

You can see it would be quite impossible to tell the story of every refugee treated at our Clinic in Pusan.

It is just as impossible to speak of everyone whose generosity and hard work kept the shelves filled with medicines and relief goods.

Many faces haunt my memory of those years; some names escape me, but the kindliness will never fade. The Recording Angel, however, takes no chances with a fallible memory. As St. Paul puts it, he has written those names in the Book of Life.

To the thousands—soldiers, sailors, officers and men, folks at home, clergymen of all Faiths, earnest workers who sacrificed their time and wallets to give material and spiritual help—to these thousands permit me to give thanks in the name of all the Sisters and all the suffering Korean people. May God bless them all!

SISTER MARY MERCY of Maryknoll.

Nihil Obstat

JOHN A. GOODWINE, J.C.D.

CENSOR LIBRORUM

Imprimatur

✠FRANCIS CARDINAL SPELLMAN

ARCHBISHOP OF NEW YORK

The *Nihil Obstat* and *Imprimatur* are official declarations that a book or pamphlet is free of doctrinal or moral error. No implication is contained therein that those who have granted the *Nihil Obstat* and *Imprimatur* agree with the contents, opinions or statements expressed.